PARALLELS:

Artists

Oriole Farb Feshbach   Claire Heimarck   Lucy D. Rosenfeld

Poets

Jeanette Adams, Margaret Atwood, Judith Berke, Gwendolyn Brooks, Virginia Cerenio,
Lorna Dee Cervantes, Marilyn Chin, Amy Clampitt, Lucille Clifton, Judith Ortiz Cofer,
Jane Cooper, Diane diPrima, Hilda Doolittle, Rita Dove, Tess Gallagher, Jorie Graham,
Emily Grosholz, Anne Halley, Joy Harjo, Penny Harter, Colette Inez, Helene Johnson,
Marjorie Keyishian, Maxine Kumin, Dilys Laing, Anne Lauterbach, Denise Levertov, Mina Loy,
Marianne Moore, Pat Mora, Erika Mumford, Joyce Carol Oates, Sharon Olds, Alicia Ostriker,
Marge Piercy, Adelia Prado, Adrienne Rich, Jane Rohrer, Muriel Rukeyser, May Sarton,
Anne Sexton, Cathy Song, Luci Tapahonso, Mona Van Duyn, Alice Walker,
Roberta Hill Whiteman, Mitsuye Yamada

Foreword by **Grace Glueck**   Introduction by **Mary Ann Caws**

MIDMARCH ARTS PRESS
New York

Library of Congress Catalog Card Number 93-77571
ISBN 1-87765-14-8

Published in 1993 by
Midmarch Arts Press
300 Riverside Drive
New York, New York 10025

Printed and bound in the United States

To Our Parents

Nettie and Louis Horch
Freda and Joe Gunderson
Anne and Morris Davidson

Contents

Foreword

Artists and poets are always invading each other's turf, and why not? Both are visionaries, wanting to extend the world beyond the tight confines of ordinary life. The images made by artists have often stimulated poets; think of Auden's Bruegel-inspired lines on the fall of Icarus in his poem, "Musée des Beaux Arts." And poets' lines have haunted artists; to wit, the death-black imagery of Robert Motherwell's painting, "At Five in the Afternoon," after the Spanish poet Federico García Lorca's elegy for a bullfighter.

In the spirit of such collaboration, the three artists of *Parallels: Artists/Poets* have "responded" to poems by 20th-century women writers, each choosing works that speak to, or challenge her own experience. The powerful image of a coiled serpent in a monotype by Claire Heimarck, for instance, addresses the poem "After Timaeus," by Emily Grosholz ("And what are we? Part snake, part crystal ball/ our hollow belly the low sounding board/ where we first hear ourselves speaking or singing/ and know we are the author of our song.").

The ancestral past is the theme of Oriole Farb Feshbach's collage-pastel, "Slow Runner," after a poem by Marjorie Keyishian. Using as a filter an adjusted 19th-century group photo, Feshbach poignantly evokes the lines about death, "Later, we hardly noticed how it plucked up old men and old women/ blurs at the edges of photos whose absence was less weighty than passing seasons/ and cousins, one had heard about but barely remembered."

And Lucy D. Rosenfeld makes a strong mix of undersea motifs, both abstract and realist, in her collage tribute to Rita Dove's "The Fish in the Stone" ("In the ocean the silence/ moves and moves/ and so much is unnecessary!/ Patient, he drifts/ until the moment comes/ to cast his/ skeletal blossom.").

But these are only three examples from a richly rewarding anthology of visual and verbal imagery. No less remarkable than the range of the poetry chosen for this project is the enterprise of the women who have put it together, and their boldness in reaching out to other minds. Enlarging on the poets' visions for themselves, they have helped to enhance the understanding of their works, and created delight for the viewer.

— Grace Glueck

Preface

Matisse has said that to be a painter one must first cut out one's tongue. Such a division of word and image has never been easy. Matisse, himself, joyfully combined them in his book, *JAZZ*, and in other collaborations as well. It is a division that runs deep in our cultural history, however. Maybe that is one reason it was so gratifying for us as artists to close the circle while working on this project.

It has been inspiring to become more deeply acquainted with these poems and poets, some previously unknown to us. Most were selected because they affirmed experiences we shared, while others both changed and challenged our perceptions. All of the poets were selected because of some felt affinity. Each artist made her own selections, resulting in a diversity of poets writing from differing places, generations, and ethnic backgrounds. Even so, they represent only a small number of the many admirable voices that could have been included. The poems we have chosen to include in *Parallels* are those that spoke especially to our own perceptions, allowing us the freedom to make our own discoveries, connections, and images. We are grateful to these poets for giving us this opportunity to find parallels within our separate forms of art and for illuminating our own lives by creatively writing about their own.

We want to thank the poets and their publishers for granting us permission to include the poems in this project. Their words are the unique threads that eventually weave a pattern common to us all. Our journey together has become much longer that we originally anticipated, and it has only just begun. We hope that our visual dialogue and the "parallels" we have discovered will reach a broad audience who will find pleasurable common ground in both the words and images.

— Oriole Farb Feshbach/ Claire Heimarck/Lucy D. Rosenfeld

Introduction

Starting Out Now Again, With Poetry

> the walk-talk slow,
> arm-in-arm
> around the world.
> > *Pat Mora*, "Mothers and Daughters"

What a starting out quality many of these poems have — how many are about roads, crossroads, and the courage of going on. And yet I don't want to put an exclamation mark there, after the courage, because these are not poems to be shouted at the top of your lungs, but rather statements to be absorbed. Alice Walker speaks of the three roads in her poem: black, white, and red; Anne Halley's "Our Journey to Ghent" forces us to pace in drifting air, and then acknowledge that "the train came and took us there, you know," for we will be forever "each other's witnesses..." about journeys, and the living they interrupt and continue. Erika Mumford's "Stopping On the Way To Badrinath" presents "a drab way-station,/ A cross-roads, not anyone's destination." Jorie Graham's "Erosion" demonstrates the way the words themselves hinge and lead on to other trains, if only we write, and read them with the time they require of us:

> ... No,
> it is our slowness I love, growing slower,
> tapping the paintbrush against the visible,
> tapping the mind.
> At times by shutting out.
> ...
> These winter joys
>
> And Snow coming tonight
> > *May Sarton*

Whatever is coming, it is what we know and hold out to each other that matters now. The intersubjective possibilities of the lyric are exhibited here, in this splendid combination of working texts, verbal and visual together. We enter here, as we may not have dared to before, into dialogue and response, all of us, poets or not yet.

There is a pattern here, and it is, finally, not just what I have been looking for, but what makes sense, for each of us, all of us, of the ongoing project we are involved in here.

> Passion is work
> that retrieves us
> lost stitches. It makes a pattern of us.
> *Jorie Graham*[1]

Like quilting together, or singing, or speaking — this ongoing conversation (like the arm-in-arm chat Pat Mora envisages as mother and daughter go arm in arm), *this* always specific yet extensible conversation is something we can hold out toward each other, spoken or written, as we start out now together again, or then, for the first time:

> Rough drafts we share, each reading
> her own page over the other's shoulder
> trying to see afresh
> *Adrienne Rich*

> — *Mary Ann Caws*

---

[1] In the final chapter of *The Music of What Happens: Poems, Poets, Critics* (Cambridge University Press, 1988), Helen Vendler shows us, quoting these lines, how Jorie Graham "does not avert her glance from the relentlessness of the search of art," and how she "continues, with her haunting and indwelling musicality, to make a pattern than constructs us as we read it." (p.458).

ORIOLE FARB FESHBACH

I have long been interested in portraiture: portraiture always grounds my work in individuals, and the stuff of their lives. Besides people, I photograph things and places from my life which can then be incorporated with found and borrowed images. I use these representational images so that they remain recognizable, but are subject to an abstract filter; and in this project, to the meaning of each poem. I choose poems that satisfy my ties to nature, art, and photography, and then research the poem and the poet for clues from which to make visual decisions. Where the subject allows, I like to use pastel for its direct, tough, yet sumptuous qualities.

JEANETTE ADAMS

For Gwen, My Mentor, My Friend

Gwendolyn Elizabeth Brooks:

gentle

generous

word-woman

daughter of Isis

lovely as a pikani lei

rare bloom citrus scent

provocative as a black sand beach

volcanic

vital

Gwendolyn Elizabeth Brooks:

dreamer

discoverer

word-woman

daughter of Isis

herstoric heroine

necessary nourishment

JUDITH BERKE

The Returner

Maybe it was the missing front teeth
but his message on my machine didn't sound
right, so when it said, I'll wait
for you in my taxi, I got afraid
and told the doorman to watch for him
and maybe send him away. So when he came
and held out the wallet I didn't even know
was missing, I was amazed
in this city, in this time
when hardly anything comes back
to you, not even your name
most times, if you give it. He had driven back
to the store and looked and looked and finally left
the message, and now was here, saying no
to a reward so peacefully
I almost hated to make him take it.
Then when I saw both of his thumbs were missing
I thought maybe he came from another
time: one of those ones
they used to call a returner:

a child would die, and the mother cut off a part
of it, so when another was born with the same part
gone, they knew it was the dead one come back—
and sometimes it was not like a baby
at all—not old, not wise exactly, just patient—
like maybe it was glad just to be back, living.
Anyway, he wasn't. He was William Smithee from northern
Florida, and when I asked why did he return
it, he said the money would be red
in his mind, like trouble. He talked to the sky
about it, I think he said, though the sky moved so fast
then, it was just another thing
to me, like the weather, the front door
where I lived, the missing part of the taxi.

GWENDOLYN BROOKS

Sadie and Maud

Maud went to college.
Sadie stayed at home.
Sadie scraped life
With a fine-tooth comb.

She didn't leave a tangle in.
Her comb found every strand.
Sadie was one of the livingest chits
In all the land.

Sadie bore two babies
Under her maiden name.
Maud and Ma and Papa
Nearly died of shame.
Every one but Sadie
Nearly died of shame.

When Sadie said her last so-long
Her girls struck out from home.
(Sadie had left as heritage
Her fine-tooth comb.)

Maud, who went to college,
Is a thin brown mouse.
She is living all alone
In this old house.

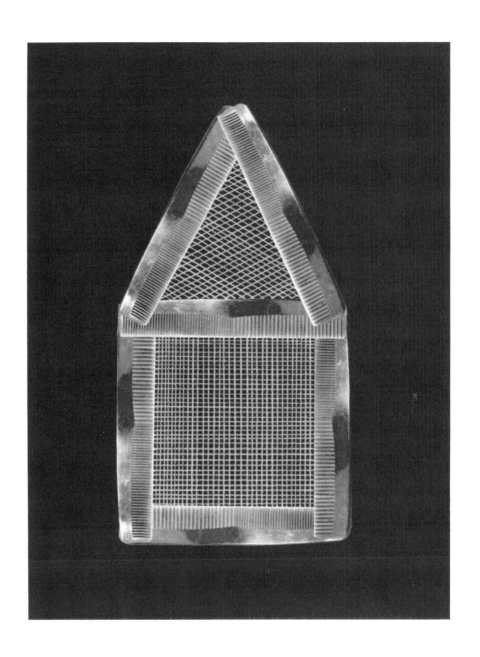

VIRGINIA CERENIO

the dream

these few moments of silence
is what i live for everyday
the blank page is the emptiness
i discover after erasing the meetings
cancelled appointments
deadlines passed
proposals that died from the birthing
of the first paragraph

i dream of white rooms like this
full of sunlight and nothing else
not even shadow or line
to mar its emptiness.
each day i wait, yearning to fill this blank page
this empty room in my heart.

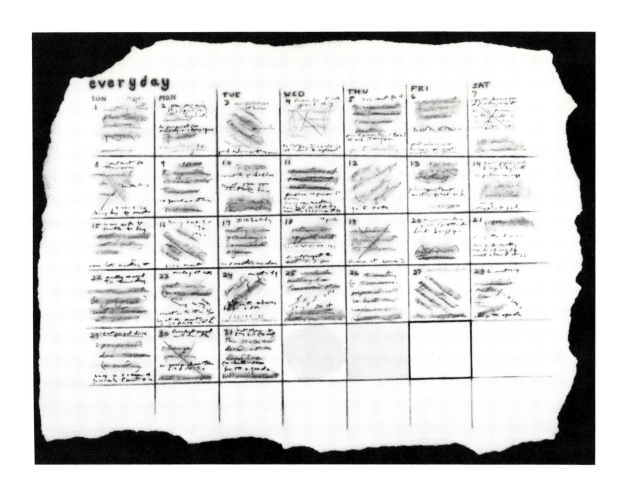

AMY CLAMPITT

Amherst

May 15, 1987

The oriole, a charred and singing coal,
still burns aloud among the monuments,
its bugle call to singularity the same
unheard (she wrote) as to the crowd,
this graveyard gathering, the audience
                    she never had.

Fame has its own dynamic, its smolderings
and ignitions, its necessary distance:
Colonel Higginson, who'd braved the cannon,
admitted his relief not to live near such
breathless, hushed excess (you cannot
                    fold a flood,

she wrote, and put it in a drawer), such
stoppered prodigies, compressions and
devastations within the atom—*all this
world contains: his face*—the civil
wars of just one stanza. A universe
                    might still applaud,

the red at bases of the trees (she wrote)
like mighty footlights burn, God still
look on, his badge a raised hyperbole—
inspector general of all that carnage,
those gulfs, those fleets and crews
                    of solid blood:

the battle fought between the soul and No
One There, no one at all, where cities
ooze away: unbroken prairies of air
without a settlement. On Main Street
the hemlock hedge grows up untrimmed,
                    the light that poured

in once like judgement (whether it was noon
at night, or only heaven at noon, she wrote,
she could not tell) cut off, the wistful,
the merely curious, in her hanging dress discern
an ikon; her ambiguities are made a shrine,
                    then violated;

we've drunk champagne above her grave, declaimed
the lines of one who dared not live aloud.
I thought of writing her (Dear Emily, though,
seems too intrusive, Dear Miss Dickinson too prim)
to ask, not without irony, what, wherever she
        is now, is made

of all the racket, whether she's of two minds
still; and tell her how on one cleared hillside,
an ample peace that looks toward Norwottuck's
unaltered purple has been shaken since
by bloodshed on Iwo Jima, in Leyte Gulf
        and Belleau Wood.

AMY CLAMPITT

The Reedbeds of the Hackensack

Scummed maunderings that nothing loves but reeds,
Phragmites, neighbors of the greeny asphodel
that thrive among the windings of the Hackensack,
collaborating to subvert the altogether ugly
though too down-to-earth to be quite fraudulent:
what's landfill but the backside of civility?

Dreckpot, the Styx and Malebolge of civility,
brushed by the fingering plumes of beds of reeds:
Manhattan's moat of stinks, the rancid asphodel
aspiring from the gradually choking Hackensack,
ring-ditch inferior to the vulgar, the snugly ugly,
knows-no-better, fake but not quite fraudulent:

what's scandal but the candor of the fraudulent?
Miming the burnish of a manicured civility,
the fluent purplings of uncultivated reeds,
ex post cliché survivors like the asphodel,
drink, as they did the Mincius, the Hackensack
in absent-minded benediction on the merely ugly.

Is there a poetry of the incorrigibly ugly,
free of all furbishings that mark it fraudulent?
When toxins of an up-against-the-wall civility
have leached away the last patina of these reeds,
and promised landfill, with its lethal asphodel
of fumes, blooms the slow dying of the Hackensack,

shall I compare thee, Mincius, to the Hackensack?
Now Italy knows how to make its rivers ugly,
must, ergo, all such linkages be fraudulent,
gilding the laureate hearse of a defunct civility?
Smooth-sliding Mincius, crowned with vocal reeds,
coevals of that greeny local weed the asphodel,

that actual, unlettered entity the asphodel,
may I, among the channels of the Hackensack—
those Edens-in-the-works of the irrevocably ugly,
where any mourning would of course be fraudulent—
invoke the scrannel ruth of a forsooth civility,
the rathe, the deathbed generations of these reeds?

JUDITH ORTIZ COFER

Postcard Poem

It should be brief
and written in indelible ink,
so the postman's hands,
sweaty with the strain
of so many words on his shoulders,
will not smudge your message.
It should contain the expected,
wish you were here,
but no return address.
It should bear an exotic stamp
with the likeness of the martyred leader
of an underdeveloped nation, or a plea
to save a nearly extinct species
of sea mammal. Through panoramic views
of impossibly blue skies it should imply
that where you are
is the only place to be.

EMILY GROSHOLZ

On the Loss of My Mother's Jewelry

One ring was sapphire, ocean
in a circle of foam,
split diamonds. Another,
two drops of blood
rubies, a teardrop between.
As long as I knew my mother,
feared her, loved her,
her hands like emblems carried them.

Bracelets of solid gold, filagree
of leaf and stem;
necklace of little pearls, coiled gold;
brooches, pins with butterflies;
worn by her mother, grandmothers, aunts.
I have lost count
of all that was lost,
the old trove she left me in trust.

The box is empty now, like a mouth in winter,
not a pearl left, small as a seed,
no link of gold, gold dust, kernel of amber;
I have lost count
of tears shed and wasted.
The line of inheritance severed,
I never will wear again
these ornaments worn once on throat and hands
I loved, as I loved my own.

They are now laid by
in darkness which seals
lost things away, which covers
my mother as well.
Her life's treasuries
slipped from her early;
my loss is nothing to hers.
But where shall I lay it all up,
my corrupt treasure in heaven,
now that the haven is plundered?

What have her hands, emptied twice over, left me?
Memories, grief, regret,
she left me enough:
my life in its prime,
bright circle, with seeds
of blood dark at the center,
gold chains of tenderness, pain
deep blue in the heart's mirrors.
Blind eyes, look here, I still wear them.

ANNE HALLEY

Fun House

Mirrors distort nothing. They hang all
asymmetries, bulbous offenses, bases
that make a self on the preposterous wall.
Hang all my always unknowing faces
unfairly finite, to infinite spaces.
Repeat, resurrect, exist, to mock
selves met anew the same, past changes of places:
The glasshouse cannot need a lock.

There was a curly mirror in the hall
and it was framed by gilded knobs and laces
of cupidbows and flowerettes. My doll
looked just like me. Two stolid kewpie graces
we stared alike. Our mirror images chases
my realized singularity, the rag arms block
my goings down new halls, choke with embraces:
The glasshouse cannot need a lock.

This mirror knows what dull face to recall.
Out of the toychest limbo litter races
a shadowdoll whose sawdust siftings fall
around my dullard feet. The doll step traces
what progress, steps, what doll-like paces
I—measured in the mirror—dully took
and overtakes: we merge in our old stasis:
The glasshouse cannot need a lock.

Mirrors make clear analyses
and outline facts in disaffected shock.
Mere-mirroring, they state their cases:
A glasshouse cannot need a lock.

ANNE HALLEY

Our Journey to Ghent

for Peter

Taste brass in the air. Imagine
our kin who haunt the borders. Their ribs, their backs,
their shrunken sex and knucklebones the weight
inside my coat. All night we pace the siding.
We are informed, no train for Ghent today.
None tomorrow. No further information.

Snow lines the furrows
where blind thumb-faces line the track to watch
flat field, flat sky. Now forced to choose
among the narrow slats, benches, that line
a box high on the platform, travelers drift
and at long intervals, in shy, shamed speech
and tongues we do not know, inquire the time.

And you and I pace, stiff in drifting air,
debating whether we must sit or stand, but drift and stay.

My darling, reality was better. You gave the right coin
to the chapel attendant. The panels still shut, we greeted
Elisabeth and Joducus, the donors, as people
long known by sight, if across distances and no relation.
We thought the piece well-lit.

And it was opened   The altarpiece spread its wings
    we entered   to the solemn, unshorn
            Lamb of God
        the meadow, Eternity,
        and the light so steady
    this web,   the coat of blood,
    of bundled ribs   that guard, would swing
out, did swing out: such light inside the light.

That the train came and took us there, you know. We are
each other's witnesses, despite the stubborn eye
that dreams its deprivation and says no.

20

COLETTE INEZ

In Praise of Outlines

In Illinois, a state edging
the five Great Lakes that open
like petals of a flower on the map,
I see America: straight-backed bull
on the northern frontier, hindquarters in the west.
The penis in New Orleans inseminates the Gulf,
the one-legged Florida kicks up shrimp
where Cuba casts nets of phosphorescent scales.

And where Costa Rica's calf
squeezes into Panama's boot,
I step into South America,
a cone set afloat in the sea,
rippled by winds
that play the Andes like a xylophone.
Look, that fire in the llama's eye
is brushed by the light of Volans and Crux.

Antarctica: in the mirage of Queen Maude's Land
buried in snow and explorers' routes,
I Imagine I chase ghost clouds, the breath
of Amundsen, Scott and Byrd,
count horizon lines lost, time numbed in the cold.

Orchids and torpor. I muse on empires
of jade in Thailand and Vietnam. On the map
these countries are a monkey's head
sniffing the Gulf of Siam. Australia's horn
gores the Torres Straits,
Tasmania's shield is cast adrift to float
in a Tasman Sea whose shipping lines
I pretend to sail.

Dazed from invented journeys,
I close the pages of a gazetteer
in a kitchen with windows that look out
on a spray of stars in the Milky Way, advancing
from north to south like two peninsulas,
like coral reefs.

MARJORIE KEYISHIAN

Slow Runner

Remember when death was brand new,
a chick hatching wet and unlovely,
waving tiny delicate wings to dry off its feathers?

Remember when death came for one's grandma,
the absolutely beloved, smelly little woman,
whose nourishing was round, that early queen,
the shape of what really was, alchemist
of squash and corpses of chickens.

Later, we hardly noticed how it plucked up old men and
          old women,
blurs at the edges of photos whose absence was less weighty
          than passing seasons,
and cousins one had heard about but barely remembered.

Now he stands at the bottom of your bed, my dear,
Sticks to you as if you were tar paper
and he, so grey so small, grows somewhat larger every single
          day,
whether or not we pay attention.

And the conversation dribbles into coughs, shrugs.
Both you and he look out past smoky streaks at the uniform
grey of a February sky. Someone could find shapes, a
          pattern of
dark and light, delicate as fingerprints
no one particularly wants to read. Mr. Clean wipes them
          down.

Both you and he have nothing much to say.
You rage from time to time.
He swallows and hiccups.
Or visa versa.

DILYS LAING

Kwan Yin

The slanted eyes
the two hands like one flower
the raiment musical about the limbs
peace, like a quiet shower
of brief rain
bringing the noon of pain
its cool relief.

The tapers bud with fire.
The long slow hymns
rise from the carven choir,
lifting above the world
the sorrow of things human.
Hail Mary, full of grace!
Blessed art thou among women.

The white hands curled
around the heart of flame
the mantle folded like a fugue of peace
the sweet and bitter name
the pitiful eyes
the crown of Paradise
the mouth of grief.

1938 (?)

DILYS LAING

Shopping List

One ouakari
two toucans
three thrips
four foraminifera
five filefish
six silkworms
seven setters
eight eiderducks
nine nightcrawlers
ten tent caterpillars
eleven elephants
twelve twigborers
thirteen thistlecocks
fourteen foraging ants
fifteen finches
sixteen sickelbills
seventeen secretary birds
eighteen eyras
nineteen nightingales
twenty twitlarks

Charge them please

Early 1930's

Memos

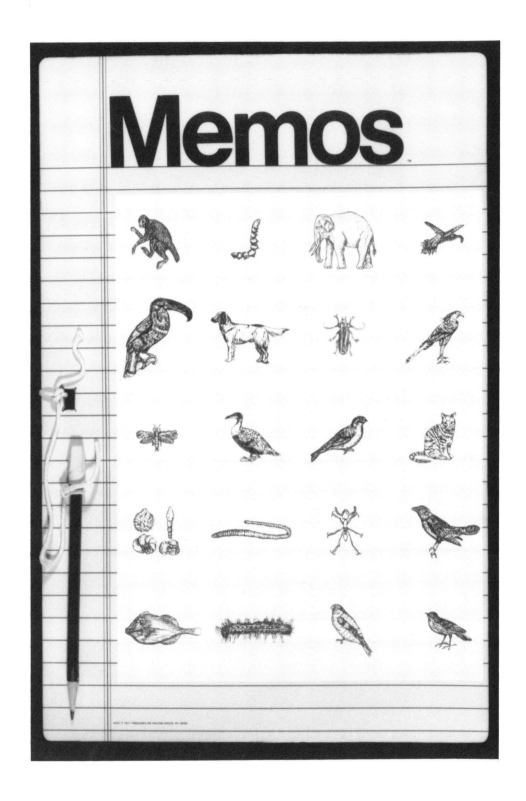

MINA LOY

Brancusi's Golden Bird

The toy
become the aesthetic archetype

As if
some patient peasant God
had rubbed and rubbed
the Alpha and Omega
of Form
into a lump of metal

A naked orientation
unwinged   unplumed
the ultimate rhythm
has lopped the extremities
of crest and claw
from
the nucleus of flight

The absolute act
of art
conformed
to continent sculpture
—bare as the brow of Osiris—
this breast of revelation

an incandescent curve
licked by chromatic flames.
in labyrinths of reflections

This gong
of polished hyperaesthesia
shrills with brass
as the aggressive light
strikes
its significance

The immaculate
conception
of the inaudible bird
occurs
in gorgeous reticence

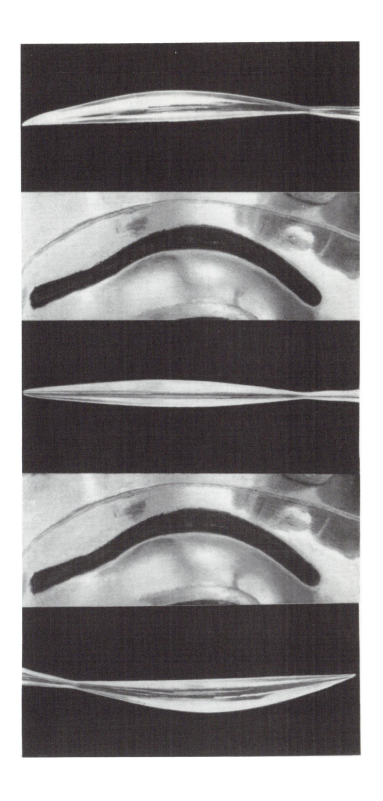

MINA LOY

Gertrude Stein

Curie
of the laboratory
of vocabulary
she crushed
the tonnage
of consciousness
congealed to phrases
to extract
a radium of the word

ERIKA MUMFORD

Gold Bangles: for Suchitra

It is twelve years since I first put on
these bangles. Circles
of yellow Indian gold,
they bruised the bones of my hand
as I pulled them on.
I sleep in them: my husband
can tell my mood
from the sound of my bangles
in the dark.

No ornaments, they are
like hair or fingernails part
of my body.
One has a raised design
or spell. The other
is plain, and dented
by my children's teeth.

Daughter, on your wedding day
I will put golden bangles
on your wrists. Gold
to keep you from want
in strangers' houses, and
for beauty: lying down naked
as on the night you were born,
you shall wear upon your dark skin
gold from this distant country
of your birth.

ERIKA MUMFORD

Stopping On The Way To Badrinath

What was somehow sad about Yogimath
Was that it was merely a drab way-station,
A cross-roads, not anyone's destination.

At sunset I climbed a thorny path
Past goats into the nearer hills.
The air was clangorous with bells

And with the unearthly rise and fall
Of the chanting of worshippers: out of the bus,
Where they had chattered like tourists, like us,

They headed straight for the nearest temple,
Safe in their pilgrimage. And I
Who wore no one's amulet — my way

Skirted a dangerous nearness to — what?
I had felt it shivering on the ghat
River-washed in Benares: a sense

Of gathering light, the crystal core
Of an almost visible energy. Here
It was something to do with a mountain presence;

Perhaps the Himalayas themselves
Are what is meant by the gods. Veils
Of ice-penumbra sweep their sides

— Or stifling avalanche shroud. In his pride
A British climber christened his child
Nanda Devi. At twenty the mountain took her,

Rolled her up in a roaring, wild
Tantrum of snow and scree, then shook her
Free of its shoulder.

                My winding trail
Gleamed past foothills black in the fall
Of ambiguous light.

Had I stayed too late?
I ran down the goat-path back to town,
To the mud-walled hostel set in a hill,

The room lit by a single brown
Candle stuck on the windowsill,
And filled with the sound of chanting, still.

JOYCE CAROL OATES

Homage to Virginia Woolf

I walked into the river and the river greedily arose.
It must have been waiting for years. It must have felt no alarm.

The finest hour of my life? — the final page, the punctuation,
the relief of escaping madness.
The solace of never being required to *begin again*.

I walked into the river and bells rang in a drunken frenzy.
It must have been a wedding, for strangers pressed their wet mouths
        against mine.
Giant fish nibbled at my toes like lovers.

An invisible woman sinking, staggering, being carried down-
        stream, heavier than one would have thought.
And far more stubborn.

A fin passing far out—look, how it turns, how it curves near!

This is the finest hour of my life, this completion.
Waves upon waves, no end to them, but no thought, no brain
        to think, no fevered beating, no voice.

(I like, I once gaily said, to go out of the room talking,
an unfinished casual sentence on my lips.)

I walked into the river and the river greedily arose.
Left behind was the racket of life!—the whirring terror of death!
The eclipse deepening around Roger's grave!
And is this War not the doom of our civilization?
I think it is. I think it must be. I do not care to survive.

But in my diary, as you all shall see, I noted *Haddock and sausage meat:*
One gains a certain hold on sausage and haddock
by writing them down.

One gains a certain hold on one's life
by boldly casting it aside.

LUCI TAPAHONSO

I Am Singing Now

the moon is a white sliver
balancing the last of its contents
in the final curve of the month

my daughters sleep
in the back of the pickup
breathing small clouds of white in the dark
they lie warm and soft
under layers of clothes and blankets
how they dream, precious ones, of grandma
and the scent of fire
the smell of mutton
they are already home.

i watch the miles dissolve behind us
in the hazy glow of taillights and
the distinct shape of hills and mesas loom above
then recede slowly in the clear winter night.

i sing to myself and
think of my father
teaching me, leaning towards me
listening as i learned
"just like this," he would say
and he would sing those old songs

into the fiber of my hair,
into the pores of my skin,
into the dreams of my children

and i am singing now
for the night
the almost empty moon
and the land swimming beneath cold bright stars.

MONA VAN DUYN

A Bouquet of Zinnias

One could not live without delicacy, but when
I think of love I think of the big, clumsy-looking
hands of my grandmother, each knuckle a knob,
stiff from the time it took for hard grasping,
with only my childhood's last moment for the soft touch.
And I think of love this August when I look
at the zinnias on my coffee table. Housebound
by a month-long heat wave, sick simply of summer,
nursed by the cooler's monotone of comfort,
I brought myself flowers, a sequence of multicolors.
How tough they are, how bent on holding their flagrant
freshness, how stubbornly in their last days instead
of fading they summon an even deeper hue
as if they intended to dry to everlasting,
and how suddenly, heavily, they hang their heads at the end.
A "high prole" flower, says Fussell's book on American
class, the aristocrat wouldn't touch them, says Cooper
on class in England. So unguardedly, unthriftily
do they open up and show themselves that subtlety,
rarity, nuance are almost put to shame.
Utter clarity of color, as if amidst all that
mystery inside and outside one's own skin
this at least were something unmistakeable,
multiplicity of both color and form, as if
in certain parts of our personal economy
abundance were precious—these are their two main virtues.

In any careless combination they delight.
Pure peach-cheek beside the red of a boiled beet
by the perky scarlet of a cardinal by flamingo pink
by sunsink orange by yellow from a hundred buttercups
by bleached linen white. Any random armful
of the world, one comes to feel, would fit together.
They try on petal shapes in public, from prim scallops
to coleslaw shreds of a peony heart, to the tousle
of a football chrysanthemum, to the guilelessness
of a gap-toothed daisy, and back to a welter
of stiff, curved dahlia-like quills. They all reach out.

It has been a strange month, a month of zinnias.
As any new focus of feeling makes for the mind's
refreshment (one of love's multitudinous uses),
so does a rested mind manage to modify
the innate blatancy of the heart. I have studied these blooms
who publish the fact that nothing is tentative
about love, have applauded their willingness to take

love's ultimate risk of being misapprehended.
But there are other months in the year, other levels
of inwardness, other ways of loving. In the shade
in my garden, leaf-sheltering lilies of the valley,
for instance, will keep in tiny, exquisite bells
their secret clapper. And up from my bulbs will come
welcome Dutch irises whose transcendent blue,
bruisable petals curve sweetly over their center.

CLAIRE HEIMARCK

This has been a very complex project. I think of a printmaker who was known for filling the borders of his etchings with an overflow of images. He said these marginalia were the birds that flew through as he worked that didn't get in the picture. I wish I could capture all the images that flew before the mind's eye while considering these poems. Some were associations to well-known paintings. The Unicorn Tapestries at the Cloisters, for example, connected in my thoughts with the poem "Sheltered Garden," by H.D.. That idea flow may not be visible in the end, but it was a motivation for the images that follow. I am happy there were so many birds to see.

FOLIO II

EMILY GROSHOLZ

After Timaeus

for Rémi Brague

The serpent is all belly, and Timaeus'
strange production nothing more at first
than radiant limbs about a living sphere
unconscious of itself, all ears and eyes
afloat in the matrix of the universe.

And what are we? Part snake, part crystal ball,
our hollow belly the low sounding board
where we first hear ourselves speaking or singing
and know we are the author of our song.

Sealed by the baleful birthmark of the navel,
we live with the necessity of evil
and breach our paradise, each time we fall
to speech, self-knowledge and the grand finale.

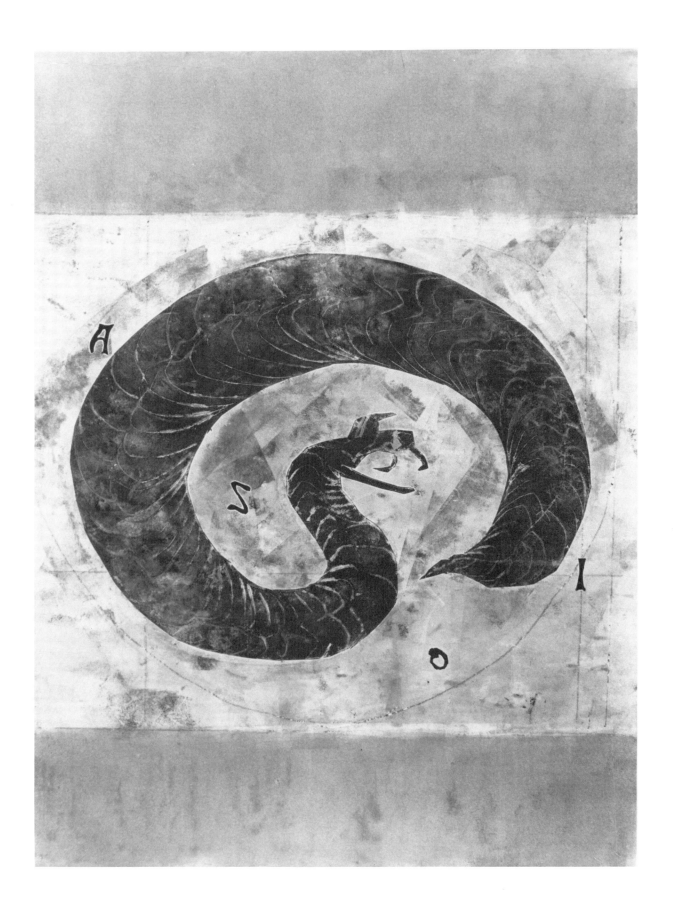

H.D.

Sheltered Garden

I have had enough.
I gasp for breath.

Every way ends, every road,
every foot-path leads at last
to the hill-crest —
then you retrace your steps,
or find the same slope on the other side,
precipitate.

I have had enough —
border-pinks, clove-pinks, wax-lilies,
herbs, sweet-cress.

O for some sharp swish of a branch —
there is no scent of resin
in this place,
no taste of bark, of coarse weeds,
aromatic, astringent —
only border on border of scented pinks.

Have you seen fruit under cover
that wanted light —
pears wadded in cloth,
protected from the frost,
melons, almost ripe,
smothered in straw?

Why not let the pears cling
to the empty branch?
All your coaxing will only make
a bitter fruit —
let them cling, ripen of themselves,
test their own worth,
nipped, shrivelled by the frost,
to fall at last but fair
with a russet coat.

Or the melon —
let it bleach yellow
in the winter light,
even tart to the taste —
it is better to taste of frost
the exquisite frost —
than of wadding and of dead grass.

For this beauty,
beauty without strength,
chokes out life.
I want wind to break,
scatter these pink-stalks,
snap off their spiced heads,
fling them about with dead leaves —
spread the paths with twigs,
limbs broken off,
trail great pine branches,
hurled across the melon-patch,
break pear and quince —
leave half-trees, torn, twisted
but showing the fight was valiant.

O to blot out this garden
to forget, to find a new beauty
in some terrible
wind-tortured place.

ANN LAUTERBACH

TUSCAN VISIT (Simone Martini)

1.

Day leaned from its agency: a false, hollow gold,
An old temporary bridge, huge trees
Bunched over the night like night bunched
Into another language —
                                        leaned, and sifted
Its warnings onto her.
It seemed to ask
Why carry these figures on your back
Why adhere when feet have already blossomed
On the slippery tile, and the carved faces
Look down, hidden and humorless because sacred.
That day was a little stung, a little ruined.
The girl had brought the weather with her
Like a toy blindly churning a smoky stench
Into the coiled trees. Yellow hedges,
Pruned into steps, where no one walked,
Where everyone had walked, were a riddle or task
Something in any case to enter willingly
As one passes into sight. The statues glared.
The bridge rattled like gunshot briefly, under pressure.
She thought of the voice she knew best and heard it arch
From side to side, stitching a canopy.
She could look nothing up.
She could only guess.

2.

It must have been early
Before light had split her unfinished skin of dream
And awakened the tumbling arc of saying —
                              In Siena, a sloped shell
                    Choreographed to wander to sleep to kiss
                    To run freely across to be sheltered
                    To eat to watch to talk —

Who is it?
It must have been early,

The ground newly splintered into grass,
Sitting on the porch, reading,
Sparrows stringing from limb to limb; early,
At dusk, swallows looping, long columns of gnats,
Bats pinching the air, dogs yapping in the courtyard,
The breeze breaching her ankles
Draped in the foreground, cool smoke
Lifting from the frame
A white scent
In which gold weather sat with gold birds
Depicting it
Who is it?

3.

A conspiracy of stars, night's umbilical blue
Shunt — details — shunt —
Looking at and being in
Have you seen my diary?
What time is it?
She twists away from her book —
What did she see?
The hills as a journey,
The sky as a sign,
Cypress beards —
It came as a subject
Lick, stamp, address
She twisted away
Shunt — details — shunt —
And stared
And startled
Disquiet, reflection, inquiry, submission, merit
Looking at and being in
A conspiracy of blues, night's umbilical star.

4.

Detained in such an arena, mute, subjected,
Consumed by what she could not know,
The trance of facts surrounding her,
Codes among the multitudes —
Would you save my place?

Flies, bees, birds
And the harbor full of boys
Sporting their nudity under other auspices,
Her love engraved like a platitude
On a charm, even her solitude — she

Hears the crest of bells
Through the patient door
Dividing her from it, it from us —
Inspired, installed, ceded.

5.

You go to a place, you stare
At the weather, naming it fondly.
You are amazed by the moon.
You say *portal* and *garment* to yourself
And notice the pressure of young fat thighs
Invested in satin. The trees
Ride in and out of the composition
And the hills, frescoed to the sky,
Are absorbed and absorbent in milky light.
You pluck stray flowers; you drink local wine,
You go to a place, you see
A woman trimmed in gold;
The women are trimmed in gold
And are not transparent.
You say to yourself *spine*,
You say *kneel, issue, wing*
As the map flies open into its depictions.
Her hand on the cowl of her robe,
Her small mouth turned down,
Her thumb holding a book open,
Her body recoiled from the offered lilies.

RITA DOVE

In the Museum

a boy, at most
sixteen.

Besieged by the drums
and flags of youth,
brilliant gravity
and cornucopian stone

retreat.
The Discus Thrower
(reproduction)
stares as he crosses the lobby
and enters
the XIVth century.

I follow him as far
as the room with the blue Madonnas.

JOY HARJO

Hieroglyphic

June, I don't have to use magic burned into roots of antelope words
to tell you what I mean when I say I met myself in the Egyptian Room

just a few days before my thirty-sixth birthday. It wasn't vertigo, though
vertigo is common in the bowels of the concrete monster. Crossing Fifth

Avenue was a trick of the imagination. It wasn't that. By the time I had
forgiven the stolen pyramidal gateway my heart had become a phoenix of

swallowed myths. They appeared as angry angels stalking the streets, who
prophesy resurrection of flowers as they tether skeleton horses, stake out

the warmest corners. I have seen them write poetry in your poetry. They'll
tell you there is no heaven or hell; it's all the same.

I have seen heaven in a woman's eyes the color of burnt almonds.
I have seen hell in those same eyes, and I have jumped.
It's all the same.

I entered that room naked except for the dream of carrying a water jar to
the river. And within that dream a crocodile cruised the grasses, watched

me dip it, then drove me down. I remembered none of it as the spin of
broken sky replaced my meager human memory. And woke up, five

years old in a sweaty army blanket on a cot in Oklahoma, to see the false
fronts of sepulchers painted with the masks of rulers, the soul

underlined with kohl, my child's eyelash a leap in time. I once again
offered my rebel spirit up to the living. And awoke, startled to cradle

my ribs of water years later in an Egyptian Room that is merely fractile of
Egypt, to take on this torture of language to describe once more what can't

be born on paper. It goes something like this: When the mythic spiral of time
turned its beaded head and understood what was going on, it snapped. All

these years I had been sleeping in the mind of the snake, June. I have to tell
this to someone.

(For June Jordan)

56

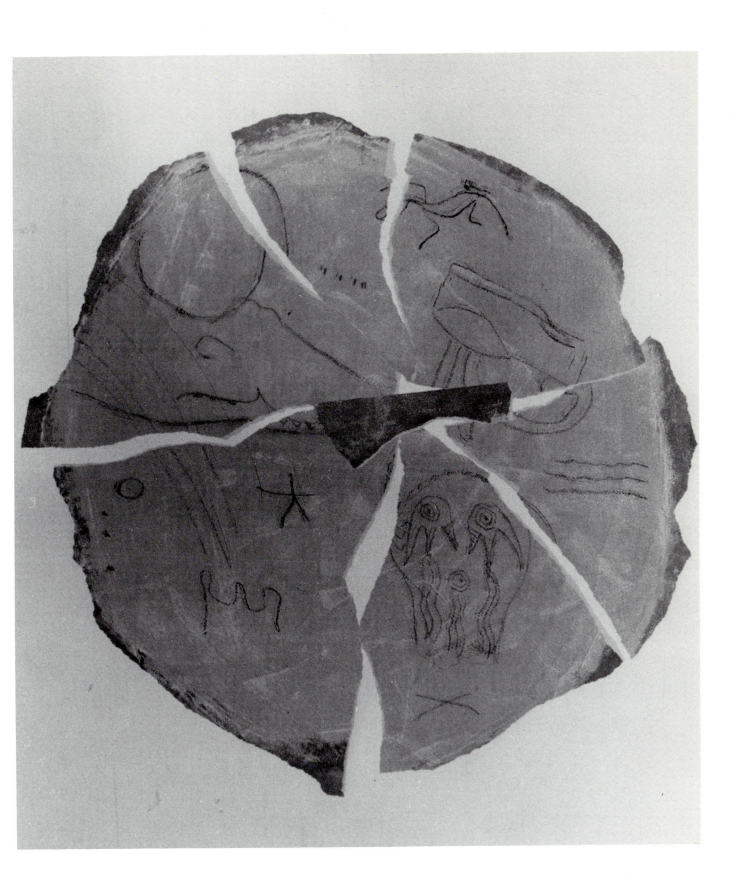

ALICE WALKER

SOME
THINGS I LIKE ABOUT
MY TRIPLE BLOODS

Black relatives
you are always
putting yourselves
down
But you almost never
put down
Africa
You are the last
man
woman
and child
to stand up
for everybody's
Mother
though so much rampant motherfuckering in the language makes one
blue
And I like that
about you.

White relatives
I like your roads
of course you make
too many of them
and a lot of them
aren't going anywhere
but you make them really well
nevertheless
as if you know where they go and how they'll do
And I like that
about you.

Red relatives
you never start
anything
on time
Time itself
in your thought

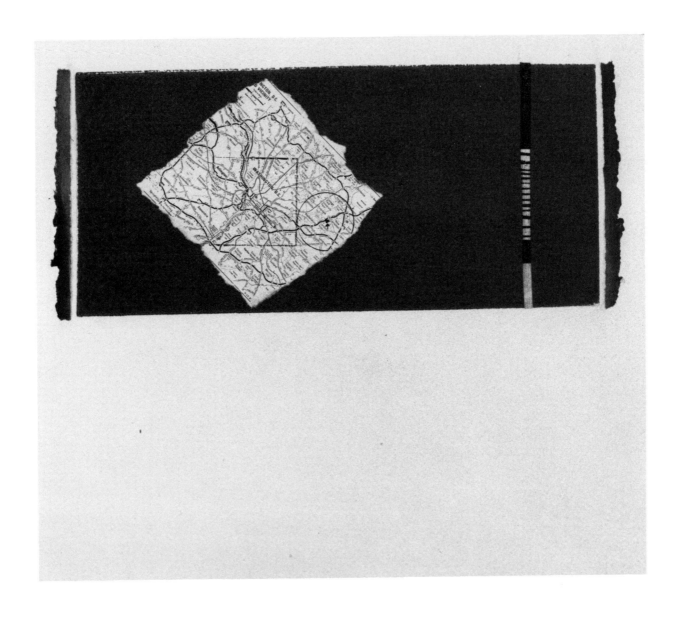

not being about
timeliness
so much
as about time*less*ness.
Powwows could
take forever
and probably do
in your view
and you could care
less.
And I like that
about you.

LUCILLE CLIFTON

water sign woman

the woman who feels everything
sits in her new house
waiting for someone to come
who knows how to carry water
without spilling, who knows
why the desert is sprinkled
with salt,why tomorrow
is such a long and ominous word.

they say to the feel things woman
that little she dreams is possible,
that there is only so much
joy to go around, only so much
water. there are no questions
for this, no arguments. she has

to forget to remember the edge
of the sea, they say, to forget
how to swim to the edge, she has
to forget how to feel, the woman
who feels everything sits in her
new house retaining the secret
the desert knew when it walked
up from the ocean, the desert,

so beautiful in her eyes;
water will come again
if you can wait for it.
she feels what the desert feels.
she waits.

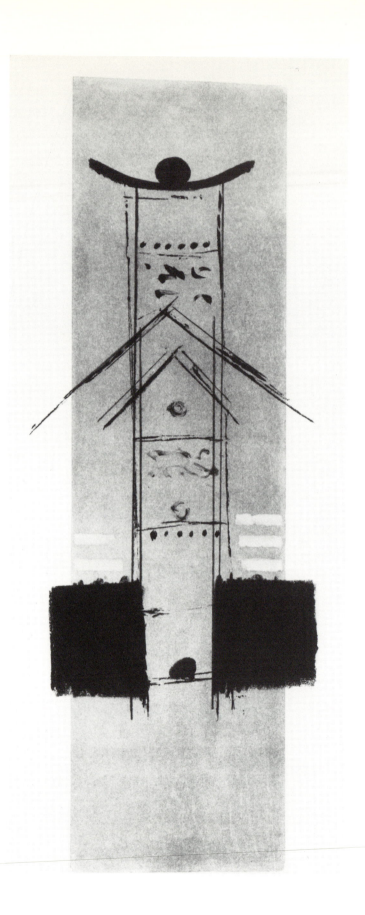

ADRIENNE RICH

Culture and Anarchy

Leafshade stirring on lichened bark
                                Daylilies
run wild, "escaped" the botanists call it
from dooryard to meadow to roadside

Life-tingle of angled light
                        late summer
sharpening toward fall, each year more sharply

This headlong, loved, escaping life

Rainy days at the kitchen table typing,
heaped up letters, a dry moth's
perfectly mosaiced wings, pamphlets on rape,
forced sterilization, snapshots in color
of an Alabama woman still quilting in her nineties,
The Life and Work of Susan B. Anthony. . . .

> *I stained and varnished*
> *the library bookcase today and superintended*
> *the plowing of the orchard. . . .*
> *Fitted out a fugitive slave for Canada*
> *with the help of Harriet Tubman. . . .*
> *The women's committee failed*
> *to report. I am mortified to death for them. . . .*
> *Washed every window in the house today.*
> *Put a quilted petticoat in the frame.*
> *Commenced Mrs. Browning's Portuguese*
> *Sonnets. Have just finished*
> *Casa Guidi Windows, a grand poem*
> *and so fitting to our struggle. . . .*
> *To forever blot out slavery is the only*
> *possible compensation for this*
> *merciless war. . . .*
>
> *The all-alone feeling will creep over me. . . .*

Upstairs, long silence, then
again, the sudden torrent of your typing

Rough drafts we share, each reading
her own page over the other's shoulder
trying to see afresh

An energy I cannot even yet
take for granted: picking up a book
of the nineteenth century, reading there the name
of the woman whose book you found
in the old town Athenaeum
beginning to stitch together
Elizabeth Ellet
Elizabeth Barrett
Elizabeth Blackwell
Frances Kemble
Ida B. Wells-Barnett
Susan B. Anthony

On Saturday Mrs. Ford took us to Haworth,
the home of the Brontë sisters. . . .
A most sad day it was to me
as I looked into the little parlor where
the sisters walked up and down
with their arms around each other
and planned their novels. . . .
How much the world of literature has lost
because of their short and ill-environed lives
we can only guess. . . .

᪣

Anarchy of August: as if already
autumnal gases glowed in darkness underground
the meadows roughen, grow guttural
with goldenrod, milkweed's late-summer lilac,
cat-tails, the wild lily brazening,
dooryards overflowing in late, rough-headed
bloom: bushes of orange daisies, purple mallow,
the thistle blazing in her clump of knives,
and the great SUNFLOWER turns

Haze wiping out the hills. Mornings like milk,
the mind wading, treading water, the line of vision blind
the pages of the book cling to the hand
words hang in a suspension
the prism hanging in the windowframe
is blank
A stillness building all day long to thunder
as the weedpod swells and thickens
No one can call this calm

Jane Addams, marking time
in Europe: *During most*
of that time I was absolutely at sea
so far as any moral purpose was concerned
clinging only to the desire to live
in a really living world
refusing to be content
with a shadowy intellectual
or aesthetic reflection

finally the bursting of the sky
power, release
by sheets by ropes of water, wind
driving before or after
the book laid face-down on the table
spirit travelling the lines of storm
leaping the torrent all that water
already smelling of earth

Elizabeth Barrett to Anna Jameson
... and is it possible you think
a woman has no business with questions
like the question of slavery?
Then she had better use a pen no more.
She had better subside into slavery
and concubinage herself, I think. ...
and take no rank among thinkers and speakers.

Early dark; still raining; the electricity
out. On the littered table
a transparent globe half-filled
with liquid light, the soaked wick quietly
drinking, turning to flame
that faintly stains the slim glass chimney:
ancient, fragile contrivance

light welling, searching the shadows

Matilda Joslyn Gage; Harriet Tubman;
Ida B. Wells-Barnett; Maria Mitchell;
Anna Howard Shaw; Sojourner Truth;
Elizabeth Cady Stanton; Harriet Hosmer;
Clara Barton; Harriet Beecher Stowe;
Ida Husted Harper; Ernestine Rose

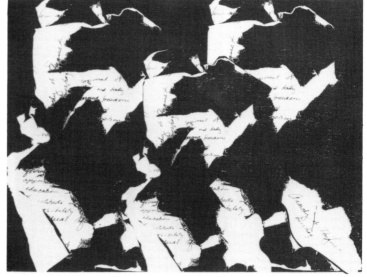

and all those without names
because of their short and ill-environed lives
False dawn. Gossamer tents in wet grass: leaflets

dissolving within hours,
spun of necessity and
leaving no trace

The heavy volumes, calf, with titles in smooth
leather, red and black, gilt letter spelling:
THE HISTORY OF HUMAN SUFFERING

I brush my hand across my eyes
— this is a dream, I think — and read:
THE HISTORY OF WOMAN SUFFRAGE

> *of a movement*
> *for many years unnoticed*
> *or greatly misrepresented in the public press*
> *its records usually not considered*
> *of sufficient value to be*
> *officially preserved*

and conjure up again
THE HISTORY OF HUMAN SUFFERING
like bound back issues of a periodical
stretching for miles
OF HUMAN SUFFERING: borne
tended, soothed, cauterized,
stanched, cleansed, absorbed, endured
by women

our records usually not considered
of sufficient value to be
officially preserved

> *the strongest reason*
> *for giving woman all the opportunities*
> *for higher education, for the full*
> *development of her forces of mind and body. . .*
> *the most enlarged freedom of thought and action*
> *a complete emancipation*
> *from all the crippling influences of fear —*
> *is the solitude and personal*
> *responsibility*
> *of her own individual life.*

ᢞ

Late afternoon: long silence.
Your notes on yellow foolscap drift on the table
you go down to the garden to pick chard
while the strength is in the leaves
crimson stems veining upward into green
How you have given back to me

64

my dream of a common language
my solitude of self.
I slice the beetroots to the core,
each one contains a different landscape
of bloodlight filaments, distinct rose-purple
striations like the oldest
strata of a Southwestern canyon
an undiscovered planet laid open in the lens

> *I should miss you more than any other*
> *living being from this earth. . .*
> *Yes, our work is one,*
> *we are one in aim and sympathy*
> *and we should be together. . . .*

1978

PAT MORA

Mothers and Daughters

The arm-in-arm-mother-daughter-stroll
in villages and shopping malls
evenings and weekends
the w a l k - t a l k slow,
arm-in-arm
                around the world.

Sometimes they feed one another
memories sweet as hot bread
and lemon tea. Sometimes it's mother-stories
the young one can't remember:

"When you were new, I'd nest you
in one arm, while I cooked,
whisper, what am I to do with you?"

Sometimes it's tug
-of-war that started in the womb
the fight for space
the sharp jab deep inside
as the weight shifts
arm-in-arm
                around the world

always the bodytalk thick,
always the recipes
hints for feeding
more with less.

JANE ROHRER

In The Kitchen Before Dinner

The winter sky past the feeder,
Beyond the wood of straight trees
And the field rising to the ridge,
Is unnervingly delicate.
But you are acquainted with the country
And you know poems. You've heard this.

Years, years and years, I've looked out
From this window, stirring —
       Straight out of the sun
       a cardinal swoops to the feeder,
       his sweep, not his shape,
       the unstrokable wing of art.
Seeing that,
I want to tell you:
       The sun of poems is on the snow
       on the slope past the wood
       to the pond. What I see at 5:00.
       It marries the music from my living room.
       It is not that simple.
       I cannot explain it.
Saying that,
I think I cannot ever leave.
I'm grounded by attachment, I'm rapacious
For facts: That bowl.
       His gloves on the chair
       holding each other.
These I can explain.

TESS GALLAGHER

Second Language

Outside, the night is glowing
with earth and rain, and you
in the next room take up
your first language.
All day it has waited
like a young girl in a field.
Now she has stood up
from the straw-flattened circle
and you have taken her glance
from the hills.

The words come back.
You are with yourself again
as that child who gave up the spoon,
the bed, the horse to its colors
and uses. There is yet no hint
they would answer to anything else
and your tongue does not multiply the wrong,
the stammer calling them back
and back.

You have started the one word
again, again as though it had to be made
a letter at a time
until it mends itself into saying.
The girl is beside you as lover or mother or
the aunt who visited with a kindly face
and the story of your mother
as a girl in a life before you.

She leads you across that field
to where the cows put down their wet lips
to the rust-dry trough.
But before you can get there
it will have changed. The water
will have two names
in and out of the ground. The song
you are singing, its familiar words and
                    measures,
will be shadowed and bridged.

Remember the tune for the words.
Remember the cows for the field, those
in their sacred look who return
their great heads to the centuries of grass.

Out of sleep you are glad
for this rain, are steadied by my staying awake.
The trough will fill
and it will seem as though the dream
completes its far side.

To speak is to be robbed and clothed,
this language always mine
because so partly yours. Each word
has a crack in it to show the strain
of all it holds, all that leaks
away. Silent now, as when another
would think you sullen or
absent, you smoke after a meal, the sign
of food still on the plate, the two
chairs drawn away and angled again
into the room.

The rain enters, repeating its single word
until our bodies in their store-bought clothes
make a sound against us, the dangerous visit
of the flesh perfecting its fears
and celebrations, drinking us in
by the slow unspeakable syllables

I have forced up the screen
and put out the palm of my hand past the rush
of the eaves. In the circular glow of the porch
the lighted rain is still, is falling.

MAY SARTON

A Winter Notebook

1

Low tide —
The sea's slow motion,
The surge and slur
Over rocky shingle.

A few gulls ride
Rocking-horse waves.

Under blurred gray sky
The field shines white.

2

I am not available
At the moment
Except to myself.

Downstairs the plumber
Is emptying the big tank,
Water-logged.
The pump pumped on and on
And might have worn out.

So many lives pour into this house,
Sometimes I get too full;
The pump wears out.

So now I am emptying the tank.
It is not an illness
That keeps me from writing.
I am simply staying alive
As one does
At times by taking in,
At times by shutting out.

3

I wake in a wide room
Before dawn,
Just a little light framed by three windows.
I wake in a large space
Listening to the gentle hush of waves.

I watch the sea open like a flower
A huge blue flower

As the sun rises
Out of the dark.

4

It is dark when I go downstairs
And always the same shiver
As I turn on the light —
There they are, alive in the cold,
Hyacinths, begonias,
Cyclamen, a cloud of bloom
As though they were birds
Settled for a moment in the big window.

I wake my hand, still half asleep,
With a sweet geranium leaf.

After breakfast
I tend to all their needs,
These extravagant joys,
Become a little drunk on green
And the smell of earth.

We have lived through another
Bitter cold night.

5

On this dark cold morning
After the ice storm
A male pheasant
Steps precisely across the snow.

His red and gold,
The warmth and shine of him
In the white freeze,
Explosive!
A firecracker pheasant
Opens the new year.

6

I sit at my desk under attack,
Trying to survive
Panic and guilt, the flu . . .

Outside
Even sunlight looks cold
Glancing off glare ice.

Inside,
Narcissus in bloom,
And a patch of sun on the pile
Of unanswered letters.

I life my eyes
To the blue
Open-ended ocean.
Why worry?
Some things are always there.

7

The ornamental cherry
Is alive
With cedar waxwings,
Their dandy crests silhouetted
Against gray sky.

They are after cherries,
Dark-red jewels
In frozen clusters
On the asymmetrical twigs.

In the waste of dirty snow
The scene is as brilliant
As a Rajput painting.

I note the yellow-banded tail feathers,
A vermilion accent on the wing —
What elegance!

8

The dark islands
Float on a silvery sea.
I see them like a mirage
Through the branches of the great oak.
After the leaves come out
They will be gone —
These winter joys

And snow coming tonight.

73

JORIE GRAHAM

Erosion

I would not want, I think, a higher intelligence, one
simultaneous, cut clean
of sequence. No,
it is our slowness I love, growing slower,
tapping the paintbrush against the visible,
tapping the mind.
We are, ourselves, a mannerism now,
having fallen
out of the chain
of evolution.
So we grow fat with unqualified life.
Today, on this beach,
I am history to these fine
pebbles. I run them
through my fingers. Each time
some molecules rub off
evolving into
the invisible. Always
I am trying to feel
the erosion — my grandfather, stiffening
on his bed, learning
to float on time, his mind like bait presented
to the stream ongoing, or you, by my side,
sleep rinsing you always a little less
clean, or daily
the erosion
of the right word, what it shuts,
or the plants coming forth as planned out my window, row
after row, sealed
into here. . . .
I've lined all our wineglasses up on the sill,
a keyboard, a garden. Flowers of the poles
I'm gifting each with a little less water.
You can tap them
for music.
Outside the window it's starting to snow.
It's going to get colder.
The less full the glass, the truer
the sound.
This is my song
for the North
coming towards us.

SHARON OLDS

Birthday Poem for My Grandmother

(for L.B.M.C., 1890-1975)

I stood on the porch tonight — which way do we
face to talk to the dead?   I thought of the
new rose,   and went out over the
grey lawn — things really
have no color at night.   I descended
the stone steps,   as if to the place where one
speaks to the dead.   The rose stood
half-uncurled,   glowing white in the
black air.   Later I remembered
your birthday.   You would have been ninety and getting
roses from me.   Are the dead there
if we do not speak to them?   When I came to see you
you were always sitting   quietly in the chair,
not knitting,   because of the arthritis,
not reading,   because of the blindness,
just sitting.   I never knew how you
did it or what you were thinking.   Now I
sometimes sit on the porch,   waiting,
trying to feel you there like the colors of the
flowers in the dark.

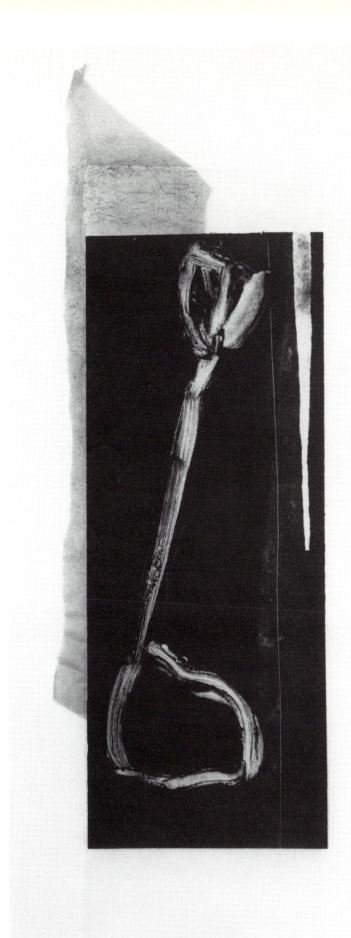

MITSUYE YAMADA

Obon: Festival of the Dead

On the day of the festival Uncle leads our procession snapping his kimono sleeves as he swings his arms. My cousins and I carry fresh-smelling wooden buckets filled with garden flowers over our arms like picnic baskets. Aunty motions to me with the broom and rake in both hands, hurrying me along as I lag behind on new wooden *getas*.

At the gravesite together we scrub the family headstone, weed, sweep and rake the ground around under Aunty's firm command and Cousin Fumiko whispers in my ear she is not my real mother, my real *Okaasan* is here, we are taking her home today.

I watch the only Aunty I know who is arranging masses of flowers about the grave in slow motion until Uncle in quaint country dialect barks "*Sorede yoka.*" That's enough. He kneels at the grave and in formal language reserved only, I suppose, for deceased wives says "*Omukae ni kimashita, sa-a sa-a ikimasho.*" We have come to take you home. Come, come, let us go.

I am told to cup my hands behind my back to carry *Obasan* home. At nine I feel too old for childish games but I play anyway. I am the only child here. In America her name will be read on Sunday during Prayers for the Dead but over here I am trying to balance the spirit of *Obasan* on my back clattering over pebbled roads back to the village.

We entertain *Obasan* royally all day on this sweltering August day. Aunty has prepared her rival's favorite dishes: *udon,* steaming hot noodles in clear soup; *imo,* sweet potatoes baked on hot charcoals; and *omanju,* sweet dumplings. Her place is set with chopsticks on the left side. Uncle says she was a "*wagamama no onna,*" a self-centered woman, but my Cousin Fumiko shakes her head, her eyes glistening and says, "She was only left-handed." I make a note of this in my mind to tell my left-handed brother back home in America "Believe it or not way over there in Japan we had one maverick aunty who used chopsticks with her left hand too!"

After dinner we take *Obasan's* treasured silk *kimonos* out of tissue papers. We girls are transformed into singing, dancing maidens. Cousin Fumiko teaches us *Obasan's* favorite songs and dances. We make a place for her and play her favorite games. When she loses, my cousin whines just like her late mother, "*Kuyashii, kuyashii,*" I hate it, I hate it. Aunty and I, strangers together, have come to know the real *Obasan* on this day, *Obon,* Festival of the Dead.

At dusk we carry *Obasan* on a handcrafted boat to the beach and join a hundred other villagers with their own dead. The priests in tall hats and white robes standing knee-deep in water chant their blessings over our vessels. *Obasan's* boat lists and sways in the water from the weight of too many *omanju* we had loaded for her long journey back to her place of rest. Uncle lights the torch on the bow and pushes her out as he coaxes "*Ike, ike,*" Go on, go on. Her sharp bow cuts the water as she joins the shoal of lights out to sea.

My cousins call out "*Sayonara Okaasan matta rainen ni neh?*" Goodbye Mother until next year? Aunty dabs her eyes with her handkerchief says, "*Anta shiawase da neh?*" Aren't you lucky? I nod in confusion. The sky is aflame as thousands of silent Roman candles float out with the tide.

MARIANNE MOORE

What Are Years?

    What is our innocence,
what is our guilt? All are
    naked, none is safe. And whence
is courage: The unanswered question,
the resolute doubt —
dumbly calling, deafly listening — that
is misfortune, even death,
       encourages others
       and in its defeat, stirs

    the soul to be strong? He
sees deep and is glad, who
    accedes to mortality
and in his imprisonment rises
upon himself as
the sea in a chasm, struggling to be
free and unable to be,
       in its surrendering
       finds it continuing.

    So he who strongly feels,
behaves. The very bird,
    grown taller as he sings, steels
his form straight up. Though he is captive,
his mighty singing
says, satisfaction is a lowly
thing, how pure a thing is joy.
       This is mortality,
       this is eternity.

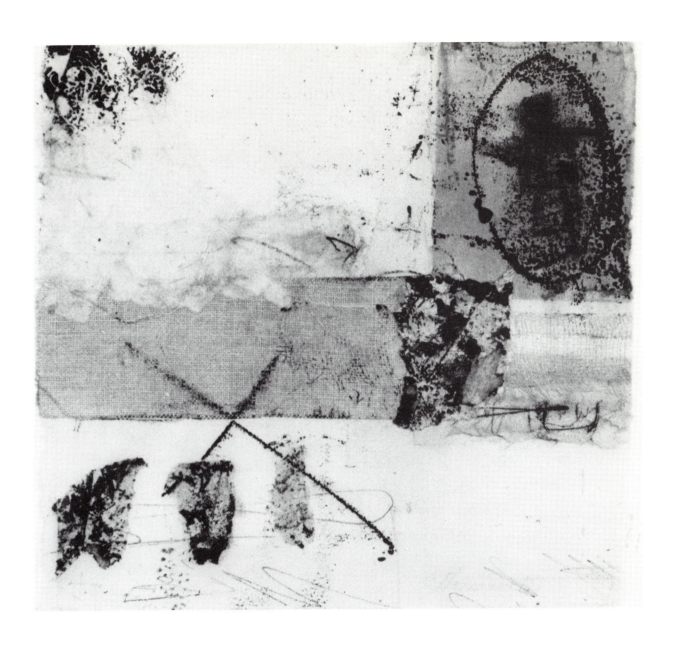

DENISE LEVERTOV

A Blessing

For Joanna Macy

'Your river is in full flood,' she said,
'Work on — use these weeks well!'
She was leaving, with springy step, a woman
herself renewed, her life risen
up from the root of despair she'd
bent low to touch,
risen empowered. Her work now
could embrace more: she imagined anew
the man's totem tree and its taproot,
the woman's chosen lichen, patiently
composting rock, another's
needful swamp, the tribal migrations —
swaying skeins rotating their leaders,
pace unflagging — and the need
of each threatened thing
to be. She had met
with the *council*
of all beings.
                              'You give me
my life,'she said to the just-written poems,
long-legged foals surprised to be standing.

The poet waving farewell
is not so sure of the river.
Is it indeed
strong-flowing, generous? Was there largesse
for alluvial, black, seed-hungry fields?
Or had a flash-flood
swept down these tokens
to be plucked ashore, rescued
only to watch the waters recede
from stones of an arid valley?
But the traveler's words
are leaven. They work in the poet.
The river swiftly
goes on braiding its heavy tresses,
brown and flashing,
as far as the eye can see.

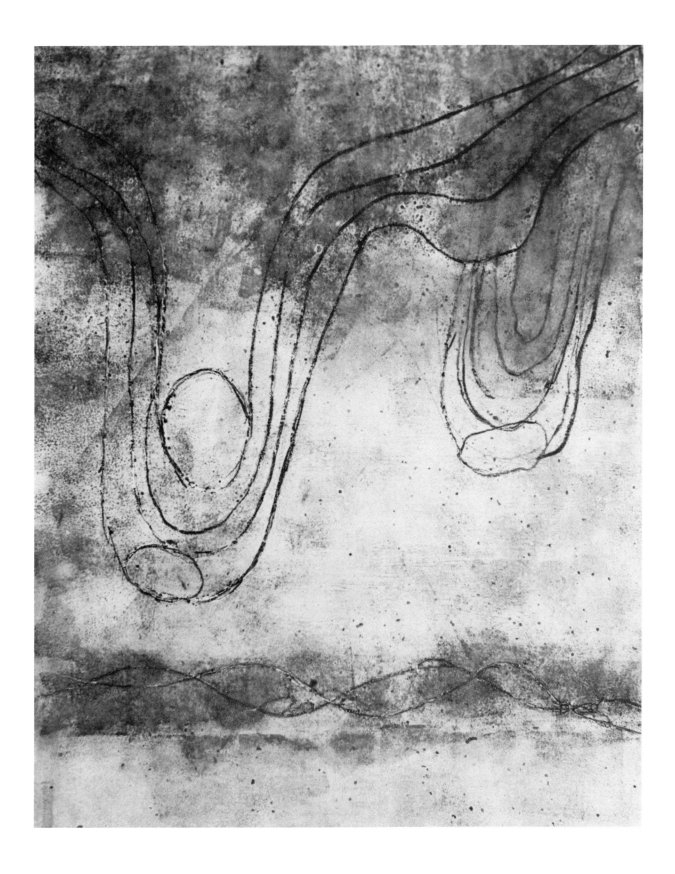

MARGARET ATWOOD

Journey to the Interior

There are similarities
I notice: that the hills
which the eyes make flat as a wall, welded
together, open as I move
to let me through; become
endless as prairies; that the trees
grow spindly, have their roots
often in swamps; that this is a poor country;
that a cliff is not known
as rough except by hand, and is
therefore inaccessible. Mostly
that travel is not the easy going
from point to point, a dotted
line on a map, location
plotted on a square surface
but that I move surrounded by a tangle
of branches, a net of air and alternate
light and dark, at all times;
that there are no destinations
apart from this.

There are differences
of course: the lack of reliable charts;
more important, the distraction of small details:
your shoe among the brambles under the chair
where it shouldn't be; lucent
white mushrooms and a paring knife
on the kitchen table; a sentence
crossing my path, sodden as a fallen log
I'm sure I passed yesterday
                              (have I been
walking in circles again?)

but mostly the danger:
many have been here, but only
some have returned safely.

A compass is useless; also
trying to take directions
from the movements of the sun,

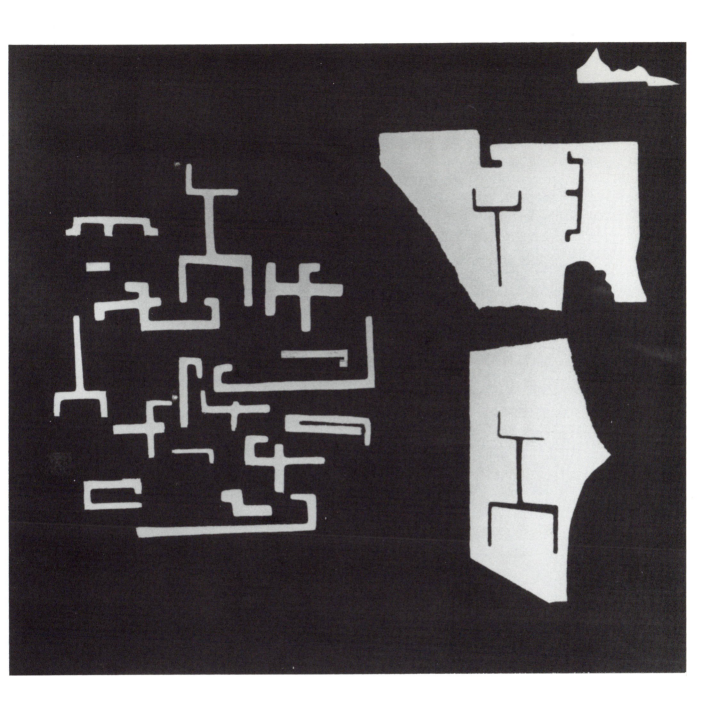

which are erratic;
and words here are as pointless
as calling in a vacant
wilderness.

        Whatever I do I must

keep my head. I know
it is easier for me to lose my way
forever here, than in other landscapes

ADELIA PRADO

Before Names

I don't care about the word, that commonplace.
What I want is the grand chaos that spins out syntax,
the obscure birthplace of "of," "otherwise,"
"nevertheless," and "how," all those inscrutable
crutches I walk on.
Who understands language understands God,
Whose Son is the Word. It kills you to understand.
Words only hide something deeper, deaf and dumb,
something invented to be silenced.
In moments of grace, rare as they are,
you'll be able to snatch it out: a live fish
in your bare hand.
Pure terror.

MARILYN CHIN

The Narrow Roads of Oku

after Basho

1.

Some steer a boat across the ocean,
Some ride a horse to its grave,
Your horse may be bold,
Your sails slim,
But better men have lost their way.
I, too, could not resist the wind.
It bends me forward, backward
All night long.
By the time the cocks call
I'll be long gone.
Patched my underwear, corded my hat,
Rubbed moxa on my legs.
What's good for the body
Is good for the soul.
The moons are lovely at Matsushima.
The fish are jumping at Matsushima Bay.

2.

Stranger, I sell you this house —
This weathermauled skeleton
Behind a shaggy head of weed.
You can have your wife, your daughter,
        her gewgaws
For my name is Basho.
I have no wife to feed,
No kindling to drag.
I'll tack-tack this rice paper on your door
For my name is Basho.
Let my stanzas flap in the wind,
My noble flags of distinction.

3.

Twenty-seventh of the third month,
Faint dawn sky.
Yonder old man Fuji
Pokes out his hoary head.

I'll miss Ueno and Yanaka, family and friends.
I'll miss your cherry-blossoms, your flushed cheeks.
How can words express my sorrow?

Either the wind stopped
Or the trees just turned to stone.

4. (. . . At the "Cloud of Dreams,"an inn near Mt. Nikko)

My name is Buddha, Buddha Grosemon,
My personal name is Gozo,
But too many grrs are bad for the throat.
You ask about my house, how can it be so clean
Without a woman? And wasn't your bed comfortable,
No horsepiss near your pillow? No lice
To confuse your head?

Who could reject my cottage, my "Cloud of Dreams?"
this cloud is not just any cloud;
Its vagueness eludes me;
Its vastness diminishes me;
Its rewards humble me.

Each day I do my chores,
Talk to the Gods through the sycamores.
There is never enough for the divine;
They are greedy and my brethren are thin.

Only once I meditated on the possibility of death.
(Dreamt of termites in rotting hulls.)
It's been ten days since Master Wright —
Well its all splendid, it's all terrible.
Some saw him clambering up a rainbow to heaven;
Those at his bedside saw death slither up
From his voicebox to his tongue.
What is poetry which cannot speak?

Today, the disciples played the deathknell,
Not a solemn tai-tai-tai-tai,
But an angry voom-voom-voom-voom.
And I, the innkeeper, could control neither
the volume nor the tempo —
Good old Basho, turtle's egg,
So, you call yourself "Monk of the Ages,"
I won't complain about "unhappy,"
If you don't pine about "sad."

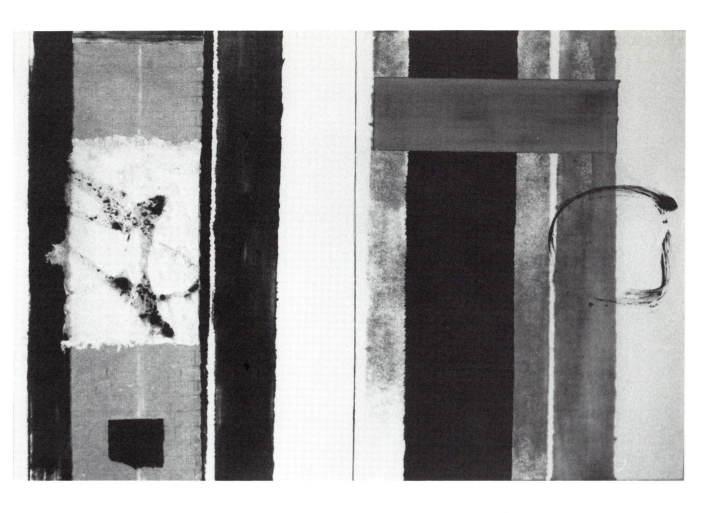

5.

Autumn is coming —
My heart, a ragged house
With four and a half mats.

I prop my head against a stone
And take a nap
For the rest of summer.

In dream, the City of Nara pulses,
A thousand statues of Buddha
Whose scent is chrysanthemum.

Autumn is coming.
I wonder who my neighbors are,
And who my friends.

Remember the River Shijimi,
The small child

Crying near its brink?
Death is easier by dew,
Quicker by fire.
Who am I to pity the monkey's cry?

How the moon hangs in the sky
Like a giant sickle —
"Heaven is cruel, my son."

And I must go on.

6.

Sir, have faith in me
I am the world's smallest traveling altar.
I am the altar and its door,
The prayer and the yearning —
For the power of God enter the most humble.

Tomorrow, let us start together
For the road to Matsushima.
Who will greet us there?
Already our shadows have lengthened
To the cliff of no return.

7.

The sunset makes my hemp shirt a little brighter.
Won't you come with me?
This field is dark, our breath is white.
The farmer carrying his dead calf, pick-a-back —
He is our way back into the world.

LUCY DAVIDSON ROSENFELD

Collage — the pasting together of disparate images, colors, textures, shapes and symbols into a coherent composition — has natural parallels with poetry. Like the poet, I choose familiar symbols, and place them in new contexts to express the images of the world around me in contemporary terms. Collage can define and interpret the layered meanings in poetry with visual images — these juxtaposed images are sometimes ambiguous, beautiful, fanciful, or factual — and almost always surprising.

FOLIO III

ANNE SEXTON

The Falling Dolls

Dolls,
by the thousands
are falling out of the sky
and I look up in fear
and wonder who will catch them?
The leaves, holding them like green dishes?
The ponds, open as wine glasses to drink them down?
the tops of buildings to smash in their stomachs
and leave them there to get sooty?
the highways with their hard skins
so that they may be run over like muskrats?
The seas, looking for something to shock the fish?
The electric fences to burn their hair off?
The cornfields where they can lie unpicked?
The national parks where centuries later
they'll be found petrified like stone babies?

I hold open my arms
and catch
one,
two,
three . . . ten in all,
running back and forth like a badminton player,
catching the dolls, the babies I practice upon,
but others crack on the roof
and I dream, awake. I dream of falling dolls
who need cribs and blankets and pajamas
with real feet in them.
Why is there no mother?
Why are all these dolls falling out of the sky?
Was there a father?
Or have the planets cut holes in their nets
and let our childhood out,
or are we the dolls themselves,
born but never fed?

ANNE SEXTON

June Bug

June bug came on the first of June,
plucking his guitar at the west window,
telling his whole green story, telling —
little buzzard who is all heart who
wants us to know how expensive it is
to keep the stars in their grainy places,
to keep the moles burning underground,
for the roots are stealing all the water,
and so he pulses at each window, a presence,
a huge hairy question who sees our light
and thinks of it:
                    You are the food,
you are the tooth, you are the husband,
light, light, sieving through the screen
whereon I bounce my big body at you
like shoes after a wedding car.

RITA DOVE

The Fish in the Stone

The fish in the stone
would like to fall
back into the sea.

He is weary
of analysis, the small
predictable truths.
He is weary of waiting
in the open,
his profile stamped
by a white light.

In the ocean the silence
moves and moves

and so much is unnecessary!
Patient, he drifts
until the moment comes
to cast his
skeletal blossom.

The fish in the stone
knows to fail is
to do the living
a favor.

He knows why the ant
engineers a gangster's
funeral, garish
and perfectly amber.
He knows why the scientist
in secret delight
strokes the fern's
voluptuous braille.

LORNA DEE CERVANTES

Como Lo Siento
"How I feel (about it)."

I heard an owl at midday.
A crow flew, spiraled, drifted,
and I thought of the circle
my own life made, and how
at heart I'm a hoverer
the way I've always drifted
toward you.
Another owl lifted from the palm.
She showed me how I rose, caught
in the wind by your skin and tongue.
I feel scooped from the banks like clay,
smoked and fired by your eyes
til I ring. I'm paralyzed by joy
and I forget how to act.
I'm a shell in the cliffs.
a thousand miles from the sea.
You tide me and I rise,
and there's no truth
more simple.

JANE COOPER

The Green Notebook

There are 64 panes in each window of the Harrisville church
where we sit listening to a late Haydn quartet. Near the ceiling
        clouds
build up, slowly brightening, then disperse, till the evening sky
glistens like the pink inside of a shell over uncropped grass,
over a few slant graves.

At Sargent Pond the hollows are the color of strong tea.
Looking down you can see decomposed weeds and the muscular bronze
        and green
stems of some water lilies. Out there on the float
three figures hang between water and air, the heat breathes them,
        they no longer speak.
It is a seamless July afternoon.

Nameless. Slowly gathering. . . . It seems I am on the edge
of discovering the green notebook containing all the poems of my
        life,
I mean the ones I never wrote. The meadow turns intensely green.
The notebook is under my fingers. I read. My companions read.
Now thunder joins in, scurry of leaves.

DIANE DiPRIMA

The Belltower

the weighing is done in autumn
and the sifting
what is to be threshed
       is threshed in autumn
what is to be gathered in is taken

the wind does not die in autumn
the moon
shifts endlessly thru flying clouds
in autumn the sea is high

& a golden light plays everywhere
making it harder
to go one's way.
all leavetaking is in autumn
where there is leavetaking
it is always autumn
& the sun is a crystal ball
       on a golden stand
& the wind
cannot make the spruce scream
       loud enough

DIANE DiPRIMA

Limantour Beach II

surf riding in / spray torn off
the top. fierce manes of Poseidon's horses
outlined white against black; flying fog bank
sun sits poised above

& line of water cuts angles to the shore
where gulls line up, solemn
slumps of black / sunning
their backs.   3 pelicans fly low, clumsy

no longer in love, no longer
regretting love.   pleased to have traded
particularity of pleasure (cloisonne of yr face
turned to mine)
                    for openness of space
play of light & shade on these hills.

kids building towers in the rising tide.

H.D. (Hilda Doolittle)

Moonrise

Will you glimmer on the sea?
will you fling your spear-head
on the shore?
what note shall we pitch?
we have a song,
on the bank we share our arrows;
the loosed string tells our note:

O flight,
bring her swiftly to our song.
She is great,
we measure her by the pine tees.

MAXINE KUMIN

Whippoorwill

It is indecent of this bird
to sing at night and
leave no shadow.
I flap up out of sleep
from some uncertain place
dragging my baggage:
a torn pillow, a tee shirt
and a braided whip.

O Will, Billy, William
wherever you are and
under whatever name
this doleful bird must tell me
one hundred and forty-six times
the same story. It is
full of fear. Such shabbiness
in those three clear tones!
Pinched lips, missed chances,
runaways, loves you treated badly,
a room full of discards,
I among them.

Now the moon sits
on the windowsill, one hip
humped like an Odalisque.
In that cold light the bird
tells me and tells me.
He cannot help it, Will.
Wherever we are he sings us
backward to the old bad times.
I too am a discard
and you,
you stick in his throat.

ADELIA PRADO

Legend with the Word Map

Thebes, Midian, Mount Hor.
Sphinx-like names.
Idumea, Ephraim, Gilead.
Stories that don't demand my undivided attention.
Maps relax me,
the deserts more than the oceans
I don't dive into
because even on maps they're deep,
voracious, untamed.
How can we conceive of a map?
Here rivers, here mountains, ridges, gulfs,
or woodlands, as scary as the sea.
The legends of maps are so beautiful
they make travel superfluous.
You're crazy, they tell me, a map is a map.
I'm not, I reply.
A map is the certainty that *the place* exits;
maps contain blood and treasure.
God talks to us in the map in his geographic voice.

111

MARGE PIERCY

Skimpy day at the solstice

The whiskey-colored sun
cruises low as a marshhawk
over the dun grass.
Long intricate shadows bar the path.

Then empty intense winter sky.
Dark crouches against the walls of buildings.
The ground sinks under it.
Pale flat lemon sky,
the trees all hooks scratching.

If I could soar I could
prolong daylight on my face.
I could float on the stark
wooden light, levitating
like dried milkweed silk.

Only December and already
my bones beg for sun.
Storms have gnawed the beach
to the cliffs' base. Oaks
in the salty blast clutch ragged
brown leaves, a derelict's
paperbag of sad possessions.

Like the gulls that cross from sea to bay
at sunset screaming, I am hungry.
Among sodden leaves and hay-colored needles
I scavenge for the eye's least
nibble of green.

ROBERTA HILL WHITEMAN

Star Quilt

These are notes to lightning in my bedroom,.
A star forged from linen thread and patches.
Purple, yellow, red like diamond suckers, children

of the star gleam on sweaty nights. The quilt unfolds
against sheets, moving, warm clouds of Chinook.
It covers my cuts, my red birch clusters under pine.

Under it your mouth begins a legend,
and wide as the plain, I hope Wisconsin marshes
promise your caress. The candle locks

us in forest smells, your cheek tattered
by shadow. Sweetened by wings, my mothlike heart
flies nightly among geraniums.

We know of land that looks lonely,
but isn't, of beef with hides of velveteen,
of sorrow, an eddy of blood.

Star quilt, sewn from dawn light by fingers
of flint, take away those touches
meant for noisier skins,

anoint us with grass and twilight air,
so we may embrace, two bitter roots
pushing back into the dust.

115

MONA VAN DUYN

The Talker

One person present steps on his pedal of speech
and, like a faulty drinking fountain, it spurts
all over the room in facts and puns and jokes,
on books, on people, on politics, on sports,

on everything. Two or three others, gathered
to chat, must bear his unending monologue
between their impatient heads like a giant buzz
of a giant fly, or magnanimous bullfrog

croaking for all the frogs in the world. Amid
the screech of traffic or in a hubbub crowd
he climbs the decibels toward some glorious view.
I think he only loves himself out loud.

PAT MORA

Sweet Wine

The hurricane taught us a new breeding technique.
                    Lepidopterist

Since no wings could outrace the wind,
blind as anger that pulled waves into
clouds, hurled sand through skin and skulls,
shredded trees like tissue paper,

the gold butterflies pressed
into mango and papaya rotting
in the grasses like fruitwine so sweet
the butterflies just sucked
and sucked deep in the soft flesh
deaf to the wind as it flung houses
and snarled away.

Warmly tipsy, those winged creatures
laughed without a sound
rolled over into a sleep thick as nectar,
and when the moon rose
they tumbled all
night, silent, amorous whirls.

MAY SARTON

These Pure Arches

A painting by Chirico: "The Delights of the Poet"

Here space, time, peace are given a habitation,
Perspective of pillar and arch, shadow on light,
A luminous evening where it can never be night.
This is the pure splendor of imagination.

To hold eternally present and forever still
The always fugitive, to make the essence clear,
Compose time and the moment as shadow in a square,
As these pure arches have been composed by will.

As by a kind of absence, feat of super-session,
We can evoke a face long-lost, long lost in death,
Or those hidden now in the wilderness of oppression—
Know the immortal breath upon the mortal breath:

A leaping out of the body to think, the sense
Of absence that precedes the stern work of creation.
Now when the future depends on our imagination,
Remember these pure arches and their imminence.

CATHY SONG

Beauty and Sadness

for Kitagawa Utamaro

He drew hundreds of women
in studies unfolding
like flowers from a fan.
teahouse waitresses, actresses,
geishas, courtesans and maids.
They arranged themselves
before this quick, nimble man
whose invisible presence
one feels in these prints
is as delicate
as the skinlike paper
he used to transfer
and retain their fleeting loveliness.

Crouching like cats,
they purred amid the layers of kimono
swirling around them
as though they were bathing
in a mountain pool with irises
growing in the silken sunlit water.
Or poised like porcelain vases,
slender, erect and tall; their heavy
brocaded hair was piled high
with sandalwood combs and blossom sprigs
poking out like antennae.
They resembled beautiful iridescent insects,
creatures from a floating world

Utamaro absorbed these women of Edo
in their moments of melancholy
as well as of beauty.
He captured the wisp of shadows,
the half-draped body
emerging from a bath; whatever
skin was exposed
was powdered white as snow.
A private space disclosed.
Portraying another girl
catching a glimpse of her own vulnerable
face in the mirror, he transposed
the trembling plum lips
like a drop of blood

At times, indifferent to his inconsolable
eye, the women drifted
through the soft gray feathered light,
maintaining stillness, the moments in between.
Like the dusty ash-winged moths
that cling to the screens in summer
and that the Japanese venerate
as ancestors reincarnated;
Utamaro graced these women with immortality
in the thousand sheaves of prints
fluttering into the reverent hands of keepers:
the dwarfed and bespectacled painter
holding up to a square of sunlight
what he had carried home beneath his coat
one afternoon in winter.

MARGARET ATWOOD

Repent

Repent, says the silver cup
with someone else's name on it

Repent, says the round mirror
with its tarnished scrolls and roses

What did I ever do to you
says the passport photo
with its oblique stare,

falling to the floor
from between the pages of a book,

*Oriental Cookery
Made Easy*, to be exact.

Little ambushes,
little slivers of grief,
each in its own neat wound, like a pocket.

I could throw them out or sell them.
I could extract them from the time
left over; if I were

religious I could wear them
around my neck and pray to them

like the relics of a saint,
if you had been a saint.

MURIEL RUKEYSER

This Place in the Ways

Having come to this place
I set out once again
on the dark and marvelous way
from where I began:
belief in the love of the world,
woman, spirit, and man.

Having failed in all things
I enter a new age
seeing the old ways as toys,
the houses of a stage
painted and long forgot;
and I find love and rage.

Rage for the world as it is
but for what it may be
more love now than last year
and always less self-pity
since I know in a clearer light
the strength of the mystery.

And at this place in the ways
I wait for song.
My poem-hand still, on the paper,
all night long.
Poems in throat and hand, asleep,
and my storm beating strong!

MURIEL RUKEYSER

Crayon House

Two or three lines across;   the black ones, down,
into the ground where grass sparkles and shines;
but the foundation is the green and the shine.
Windows are drawn in,   Overhead the sun
surrounded by his crown, continually given.
It is a real place, door, floor, and windows.

I float past it.   I look in at the little children.
I climb up the straight and planted path, alone.
In the city today grown, walking on stone,
a suddenness of doors, windows, bread .and rolls.

Roads are in all I know   :   weapon and refugee,
color of thunder calling   Leave this room,
Get out of this house.   Even then, joy began,
went seeking through the green world, wild and no longer wild,
always beginning again.   Steady giving and green decision,
and the beginning was real.   The drawing of a child.

HELENE JOHNSON

Trees at Night

Slim sentinels
Stretching lacy arms
About a slumbrous moon;
Black quivering
Silhouettes,
Tremulous,
Stencilled on the petal
Of a bluebell;
Ink spluttered
On a robin's breast;
The jagged rent
Of mountains
Reflected in a
Still sleeping lake;
Fragile pinnacles
Of fairy castles;
Torn webs of shadows;
And
Printed 'gainst the sky—
The trembling beauty
Of an urgent pine.

ALICIA OSTRIKER

A Clearing by a Stream

What impels the mind to soar forth?
What makes breath start?
What causes people to speak?
Eye and ear — what god is making them live?

    Gabriel, when we were camping, we saw a deer —
        From what does not perish emerges what perishes —

A pale violet butterfly stops near me.
When its wings are closed I cannot see the color.
When it opens its wings and flies my eyes cannot

Follow its speedy fluttering trajectory.
How then can we expect to satisfy
Our hearts with seeing?

Now it's flown off, as I anticipated,
Over the stream a minute, and now has settled
Next to me again, with my sketchbook and pen.

It opens its wings partially.
Staring, I see the pink and blue pigments
Mixing on them, very faintly shimmering,

And the thin brown veins.
Each wing having two petals,
It writhes them,

Independently,
Sensually, unlike
What I expected of a butterfly.

It stands with wings half-open in thought;
Wind pushes them. Its body is solid
Violet, long and hairy, like velveteen.

Again it loops away. Do the weeds and flowers
Take it for another flower, strangely able
To float and alight? Look at that one,

They whisper, it is stemless
And rootless! Is the butterfly to the plant
As the Great Self to ourselves?

It's back. I rest my forefinger
Next to it, and it isn't afraid, it mounts
My ridged finger and walks stiffly across my hand.

132

PENNY HARTER

Reading the Tea Leaves

After winter rain
dead leaves have steeped
in the gutter.

Easter eggs dipped in this tea
would darken
to barnyard brown.

On the neighbor's lawn an inflated swan
adrift on a stake like a weathervane
wheels slowly to face us.

I bend over the puddle,
stir with one finger
the cold silt at bottom,

watching the shredded leaves rise,
swirl and settle, as if I were
shaking them in a tiny globe.

DENISE LEVERTOV

The Room

With a mirror
I could see the sky.

With two mirrors or three
justly placed, I could see
the sun bowing to the evening chimneys.

Moonrise — the moon itself might appear
in a fourth mirror placed high
and close to the open window.

       With enough mirrors within
and even without the room, a cantilever
supporting them, mountains
and oceans might be manifest.

I understand perfectly
that I could encounter my own eyes
too often — I take account
of the danger — .
       If the mirrors
are large enough, and arranged
with a bravura, I can look
beyond my own glance.

With one mirror
how many stars could I see?

I don't want to escape, only to see
the enactment of rites.

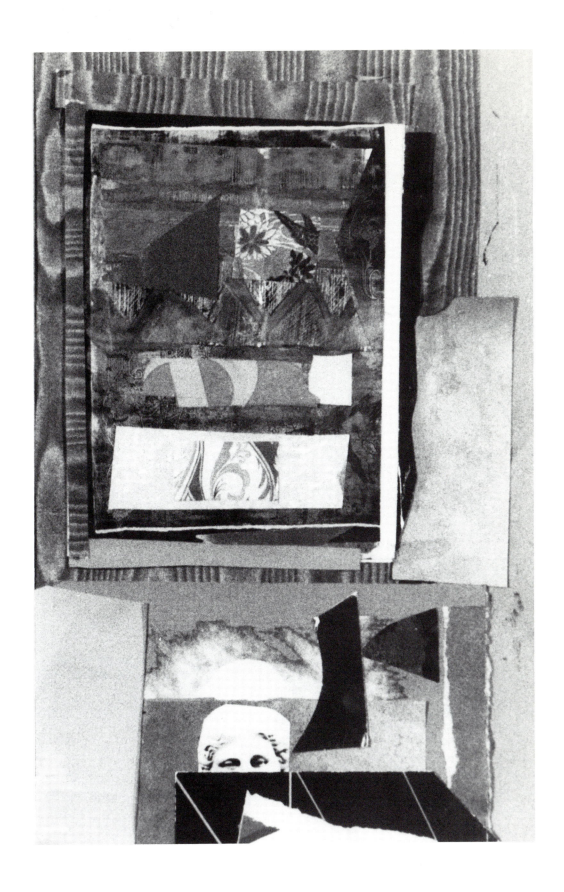

About the Poets/Critics/Artists

Jeanette Adams, a native of Orlando, Florida, is a graduate of Hunter College and holds the M.A. from City College in New York. She is the author of three collections of poetry: *Sukari*, *Picture Me In A Poem*, and *Love Lyric*, and her work has been published in several periodicals and anthologies. She has been cited for her contributions to the arts by the "I Dream A World" exhibition at the Orange County, Florida Historical Museum and was the first person to be inducted into the National Coalition of 100 Black Youth Hall of Fame. Ms. Adams is on the faculty of City College, The City University of New York and lives in Teaneck, New Jersey.

Margaret Atwood, poet and novelist, author of more than 20 books, was born in Ottawa, Canada, and grew up in northern Ontario, Quebec and Toronto, where she now lives. Her first volume of poems, *The Circle Game* (1966), won the Governor General's Award; other poetry books include *The Animals in the Country* (19680, *The Journals of Susanna Moodie* (1970), *Power Politics* (1971), *You Are Happy* (1974), *Selected Poems* (1976). Ms. Atwood is perhaps best known for her five novels, *The Edible Woman*, *Surfacing*, *Lady Oracle*, *Life Before Man*, and *Bodily Harm*, and for her two collections of short fiction, *Dancing Girls* and *Bluebeard's Egg*.

Judith Berke was born in New York City, attended Smith College, studied painting at l'Académie de la Grande Chaumière in Paris, and acting with Lee Strasberg in New York. Her first book, *White Morning* (1989), was followed by a chapbook, *Acting Problems* (1992). She lives in Miami Beach, Florida.

Gwendolyn Brooks, the first African-American to win a Pulitzer Prize (1950), was born in Topeka, Kansas, and has lived most of her life in Chicago, Illinois. She is a graduate of Wilson Junior College (Chicago) and has received over 50 honorary degrees. Ms. Brooks is a member of the American Academy of Arts and Letters, and in addition to the Pulitzer Prize has been honored with the Shelley Memorial, the Ainsfield-Wolf, and the Kumba Liberation Awards, as well as two Guggenheim Fellowships. She has published more than 15 books, including poetry, children's verse, writing manuals, a novel and an autobiography.

Virginia Cerenio is a second-generation Filipino-American whose poems have appeared in numerous publications including *Berkeley Fiction Review*, *Breaking Silence*, and *Without Names*. She lives in San Francisco, California.

Lorna Dee Cervantes, born in San Francisco, California, is founder and editor of Mango Publishing, a prominent voice in Chicano literature, and the recipient of a National Endowment for the Arts Fellowship, and the Paterson Poetry Prize for her most recent book, *From the Cables of Genocide: Poems of Love and Hunger*. She lives in San Jose.

Marilyn Chin was born in Hong Kong and grew up in Portland, Oregon. She received a B.A. in Chinese Literature from the University of Massachusetts and M.F.A. from the Writers Workshop at the University of Iowa. Ms. Chin has been awarded a Stegner (Stanford University) and National Endowment for the Arts fellowships, and is currently teaching at San Diego State University in California.

Amy Clampitt was born and and brought up in New Providence, Iowa, graduated from Grinnell College, and has since lived mainly in New York City. She is the author of several books of poetry including *The Kingfisher*, *What the Light Was Like*, *Archaic Figure*, and *Westward*. The recipient of Guggenheim and Academy of American Poets fellowships, and the John D. and Catherine MacArthur Foundation Grant, she is a member of the National Institute of Arts and Letters and one of the 12 chancellors of the Academy of American Poets. In 1992

Lucille Clifton was born in Depew, New York and educated at Howard University and the State University of New York at Fredonia. She has published seven books of poetry, including *Good Times* (1969), *Good News About the Earth* (1972), *An Ordinary Woman* (1974), *Two-Headed Woman* (1976), *Good Woman: Poems and a Memoir* 1969-1980, *Quilting: Poems 1987-1990* (1991), and more than a dozen books of fiction and poetry for children. Ms. Clifton was Poet Laureate of the State of Maryland, 1979-1982; received an Emmy Award, the Juniper Prize for Poetry, and a National Endowment for the Arts Fellowship; and was twice nominated for the Pulitzer Prize. She is currently Distinguished Professor of Humanities at St. Mary's College in Maryland.

Judith Ortiz Cofer was born in Puerto Rico, moving as a child with her family to Paterson, New Jersey. She received a M.A. in English from Florida Atlantic University and was awarded a scholarship to Oxford University. Ms. Cofer is the author of two books of poetry, *Terms of Survival* and *Reaching for the Mainland*, as well as a novel and a collection of autobiographical essays.

Jane Cooper was born in Atlantic City, New Jersey. She has been honored with the Lamont Poetry Selection award; Guggenheim, National Endowment for the Arts, Ingram Merrill, and Bunting Institute fellowships and was a beloved teacher at Sarah Lawrence College (Bronxville, New York) for 37 years. Additionally, Ms. Cooper has taught at the Iowa Writers Workshop and in the Graduate Writing Program, School of the Arts, Columbia University. An essay tracing her growth as a poet, entitled "Nothing Has Been Used in the Manufacture of This Poetry That Could Have Been Used in the Manufacture of Bread," appears in her third collection, *Scaffolding: Selected Poem*, which will be reissued Fall 1993.

Diane diPrima, a native of New York City, has been founder or editor of several literary magazines, publisher of Poets Press and Eidolon Editions, a novelist, playwright, translator and co-founder of New York Poets Theater. She has written 28 books of verse, as well as teaching the young of all ages, from poetry-in-the-schools programs to her current position on the Core Faculty at New College in San Francisco.

Hilda Doolittle (H.D.) (1886-1961) was born in Pennsylvania and educated at Bryn Mawr College. She went abroad in 1911, and never returned to live in the United States. Her first of several volumes of poetry was published in 1916, followed by *Helen in Troy* and *Hermetic Definitions*. She also published translations, essays, dramas, film criticism, and several autobiographical novels, *Paint It Today* and *Asphodel* (recently reissued by university presses).

Rita Dove was born in Akron, Ohio, studied at Miami University in Oxford, Ohio, and received an M.F.A. from the Iowa Writers Workshop. She is the author of several poetry collections including *The Yellow House at the Corner* (1980), *Thomas and Beulah* (1986), *Grace Notes* (1989) and a novel, *Through the Ivory Gate* (1992). Her awards include the Pulitzer Prize (1987) and a Literary Lion from the New York Public Library, and Guggenheim and National Endowment for the Arts Fellowships. Ms. Dove is professor of English at the University of Virginia at Charlottesville.

Tess Gallagher was born and raised in Port Angeles, Washington. She has published five volumes of poetry including *Amplitude* (1987), and *Moon Crossing Bridge* (1992), and a collection of short stories, *The Lover of Horses*. Ms. Gallagher received a National Endowment for the Arts Fellowship in 1980.

Jorie Graham grew up in Italy and studied at the Sorbonne in France, and New York and Columbia Universities, and the University of Iowa. Her books of poetry include *Hybrids of Plants and of Ghosts* (1980), *Erosion* (1983), and *The End of Beauty* (1987). She has received grants from the Ingram Merrill, the Guggenheim, and the MacArthur foundations, and the Bunting Institute, and a special award from the Academy of American Poets. She lives in Iowa City and teaches at the University of Iowa Writers Workshop.

Emily Grosholz was born in Philadelphia. She is advisory editor and contributor to the *Hudson Review*, and has published poetry and essays in the *New England Review*, *Poetry*, the *Southern Review*, the *Partisan Review*, *The New York Times Book Review*, and other periodicals. Ms. Grosholz has published several books of poetry including *The River Painter* (1984), *Shores and Headlands* (1988) and *Eden* (1992), and been honored with a Guggenheim Fellowship, and Ingram Merrill and Djerassi Foundations grants. She is professor of philosophy at Pennsylvania State University, University Park.

Anne Halley was born in Germany, received a B.A. from Wellesley College and M.A. from the University of Minnesota. She has published two books of poems and numerous short stories, essays, and some translations. Ms. Halley lives in Amherst, Massachusetts and teaches occasionally, most recently at the University of Frankfurt.

Penny Harter grew up in Staten Island, New York and Clark, New Jersey, graduated from Douglass College, and worked in New Jersey schools as a visiting poet and English teacher until moving to Santa Fe, New Mexico in 1991 to accept a position at Santa Fe Preparatory School. Her nine books of poems include *Lovepoems* (1981), *White Flowers in the Snow* (1981), *Hiking the Crevasses* (1983), and *The Monkey's Face* (1987); a chap-book, *Keeping Time*, is scheduled for publication in 1994. She has co-edited three collections of work by New Jersey authors, received fellowships from the New jersey State Council on the Arts and the Geraldine R. Dodge Foundation, and won the Poetry Society's Mary Caroline Davies Memorial Award.

Joy Harjo, member of the Creek (Muscogee) Tribe was born in Tulsa, Oklahoma and grew up there and in New Mexico. She attended the Institute of Indian Arts in Santa Fe, earned a B.A. from the University of New Mexico, and M.F.A. from the University of Iowa. Her collection, *In Mad Love and War* (1990) won the Poetry Society's William Carlos Williams Award. She has received National Endowment for the Arts and Arizona Commission on the Arts Fellowships. Ms. Harjo lives in Tucson and is an associate professor of English at the University of Arizona.

Colette Inez, born in Brussels, Belgium, has published five books of poetry including *The Woman Who Loved Worms* (1973), *Alive and Taking Names*, *Eight Minutes from the Sun*, *Family Life*, and *New and Selected Poems*. Her work has appeared in the leading literary journals and quarterlies and earned for its author the Poetry Society Reedy Memorial Award; and Guggenheim, Rockefeller, and two National Endowment for the Arts Fellowships. She is currently on the faculty of Columbia University's Writing Program.

Helene Johnson, born in Boston, was part of the New Negro Movement and one of the youngest writers of the Harlem Renaissance. Her poems appeared in magazines including *Vanity Fair* and *Opportunity* in the 1920s, when she was an active figure in literary circles. After she married she disappeared from the New York literary scene to earn a living and raise her child, and her poetry has only recently been rediscovered. Several of her poems were included in *Negro Literature*, 1963, Hill & Wang, NY.

Marjorie Keyishian was born in Brooklyn, New York and attended Columbia University. Her poetry, short stories, and articles have appeared in many journals, including *New York Quarterly*, *The Massachusetts Review*, *Ararat*, *The English Record*, *The Literary Review*, and *The New York Times*, New Jersey section. She teaches at Fairleigh Dickinson University, Madison, New Jersey.

Maxine Kumin born in Philadelphia, published her first collection of poems, *Halfway* in 1961, and since then has produced nine others including: *The Privilege* (1965), *The Nightmare Factory* (1970), *Up Country* (1972), *The Retrieval System* (1978), *Our Ground Time Here Will Be Brief*, *New and Selected Poems* (1902), *Nature* (1989) and *Looking for Luck* (1992). She has published four novels, a short story collection, and numerous children's books. Among other awards she has received *Poetry Magazine*'s Levinson and the Eunice Tietjens Prizes, the Pulitzer Prize (1973), and National Endowment and National Council on the Arts Fellowships. She now lives in New Hampshire.

Dilys Laing (1906-1960) was born in North Wales, and was educated in England and Canada. She settled in the United States after her marriage to an American. In addition to her four books of poetry including, *Another England, Birth is Farewell, Walk*

Through Two Landscapes (1949), and *Poems from a Cage*, she published one novel, *The Great Year* (1948). More than 100 new poems (of several hundred found after her death) have appeared in such periodicals as *Harper's, Hudson Review, Kenyon Review, The New Republic,* and *Poetry* among others, since 1960..

Ann Lauterbach was born in New York City and educated at the University of Wisconsin, Madison. She spent seven years at the London Institute of Contemporary Arts. After returning to New York she wrote art criticism, worked in art galleries, and taught in writing programs at several universities. She is currently a professor at The City College of New York and has received New York State Council on the Arts and Ingram Merrill grants. Her most recent collection of poems is *Clamor* (1991).

Denise Levertov was born in Ilford, Essex, England and educated at home. She became a United States naturalized citizen in 1955. Ms. Levertov has published more than 30 books including *Breathing the Water* (1987) and *A Door In the Hive* (1989); was poetry editor of *The Nation* and *Mother Jones* magazines; associate scholar at the Radcliffe Institute; and received a Guggenheim Fellowship and two American Academy grants. For the past 10 years she has taught at Stanford University.

Mina Loy (1882-1966) was born in London, England, and studied art with Augustus John, before moving to Paris, where she soon became a regular of the Gertrude Stein circle of artists and writers. After living in France, Italy, and Spain she settled in the United States in 1936 becoming a naturalized citizen in 1946. Ms. Loy's first poem was published in *Camera Work* in 1914. After that she became a frequent contributor to literary magazines such as the *Dial*, while continuing to design and paint. Among her volumes of poetry are *Lunar Baedeker* (first published in 1923, re-issued in 1958 with *Time Tables*), *Love Songs* (1981) and her prose novel, *Insel*, published posthumously in 1991.

Marianne Moore (1887-1972) was born in St. Louis, Missouri and educated at Bryn Mawr College. She taught business skills at the Carlisle Indian School, worked at the New York Public Library, and edited *The Dial* from 1925 to 1929, and lived most of her adult life in Brooklyn, New York. Her *Collected Poems* (1951) received the Bollingen Prize, the National Book Award, and the Pulitzer Prize. She published a translation of *The Fables of La Fontaine* (1954), and a later *Collected Poems* in 1967.

Pat Mora, author of three collections of poetry, concerns herself with images of life from within the framework of the Third World, writing frequently (in both Spanish and English) about her own Southwest. She is the recipient of grants from the National Endowment for the Arts and the Texas Commission for the Arts.

Erika Mumford (1935-1988) published several collections of poetry including *The Door in the Forest* and *Willow Water* (1988). She received several poetry awards, was an editor of *Dark Horse*; and lived in Cambridge, Massachusetts.

Joyce Carol Oates, National Book Award-winning novelist, short story writer, poet, and critic is a member of the Academy of Arts and Letters and the Roger S. Berlind Distinguished

Professor in the Humanities at Princeton University. Among her many books is *American Appetites, Bellefleur, The Wheel of Love* and *A Garden of Earthly Delights*.

Sharon Olds was born in San Francisco, California, received a B.A. from Stanford University and Ph.D. from Columbia University in 1972. She is the author of four books of poetry including *Satan Says* (1980), *The Dead and The Living* (1983), and *The Father* (1992). Her books have been singled out for the Lamont Poetry Selection and the National Book Critics Circle Award. Ms. Olds has received Guggenheim and National Endowment for the Arts Fellowships and teaches in the Graduate Creative Writing Program at New York University and at Goldwater Hospital in New York City.

Alicia Ostriker is the author of seven collections of verse and has received Guggenheim, Rockefeller, and National Endowment for the Arts fellowships. The latest of her scholarly works is *Stealing the Language: The Emergence of Women's Poetry in America*. She is a professor of English at Rutgers University, New Jersey.

Marge Piercy, born in Detroit, is the author of eleven novels, a play, a volume of essays and reviews, and eight collections of poetry which include *The Moon is Always Female: Circles on the Water, Stone, Paper, Knife: My Mother's Body, Available Light,* and *Mars and Her Children*. Her poems have appeared in journals such as *Transatlantic Review* and TriQuarterly. She lives on Cape Cod.

Adelio Prado has lived all her life in Divinopolis, Minas Gerais, Brazil, where she was born. She attended the university there earning degrees in philosophy and religious education. Her first book of poems was published when she was 40, and since then there have been eight books of poetry and poetic prose. Her collection *The Alphabet in the Park* (1990) was translated from the Portuguese by Ellen Watson, who also accompanied Ms. Prado on a reading tour of the U.S. in 1988. She describes herself as "a simple person, a common housewife, a practicing Catholic."

Adrienne Rich was born in Baltimore, Maryland and received a B.A. from Radcliffe College. She has published 13 volumes of poetry, including *On Lies, Secrets, and Silence — Selected Prose, 1966-1978, Of Woman Born,* and *An Atlas of the Difficult World, Poems 1988-1991*. Ms. Rich has received many honors, including the Brandeis University Creative Arts Medal, the Ruth Lilly Poetry Prize, a National Book Award, the Common Wealth Award in Literature (1991), a National Institute of Arts and Letters Award, the William Whitehead Award for Lifetime Achievement (1992), and an Amy Lowell and two Guggenheim Fellowships

Jane Rohrer was born in the Shenendoah Valley, Virginia, attended Eastern Mennonite University, Temple University and University of the Arts in Philadelphia. Thirteen of her poems have been published in *The American Poetry Review* with additional work in other academic poetry.journals.

Muriel Rukeyser (1913-1980), born in New York City, was poet, lecturer, translator, playwright, and teacher — at Vassar and Sarah Lawrence Colleges, and Columbia University. She received Guggenheim and National Institute awards; was a member of the National Institute of Arts and Letters; and served on the jury for the Bollingen and National Book Awards.

May Sarton was born near Ghent, Belgium and educated in the United States, becoming a naturalized citizen in 1924. She has written journals, novels, and poetry collections including *Halfway to Silence* (1980) and *The Silence Now* (1988). Before devoting herself to a writing career, Ms. Sarton founded and directed the Apprentice Theater in New York and Associated Actors, Inc., in Hartford, Connecticut. A fellow in the American Academy of Arts and Sciences, she has been visiting professor and poet-in-residence at many universities, and received numerous honors including Guggenheim and National Endowment for the Arts fellowships. She has spent most of her life in the New England states of New Hampshire and Maine.

Anne Sexton (1928-1974), born in Newton, Massachusetts, was author of numerous books of poetry, recipient of several major awards including a Pulitzer Prize (1967), and professor of creative writing at Boston University. Her poetry appeared in journals such as *The New Yorker*, *Harpers*, *Hudson Review*, and *Poetry*.

Cathy Song was winner of the Yale Younger Poets series competition in 1982, and has recently taught at the University of Hawaii-Manoa. Her latest book of poems is *Frameless Windows, Squares of Light*.

Luci Tapahonso, a Navajo Indian, was born and raised in Shiprock, New Mexico. She is the author of four books of poetry including *Saanii Dahataal* (1992) and her poetry has been featured on several national radio programs. She lives in Lawrence, Kansas and teaches English at the University of Kansas.

Mona Van Duyn, born in Iowa, and winner of the 1991 Pulitzer Prize in Poetry, became the first woman ever named poet laureate of the United States in 1992. Ms. Van Duyn has taught at several universities including the University of Iowa, and lives in St. Louis, Missouri.

Alice Walker, novelist and poet, was born in Eatontown, Georgia, and although best known for *The Color Purple*, which won an American Book Award and the Pulitzer Prize, and best-selling *The Temple of My Familiar*, has been writing poetry since 1965, when she traveled to East Africa and began the collection, *Once* (1968). Her most recent poetry volume is *Her Blue Body Everything We Know, Earthing Poems 1965-1990 Complete*.

Roberta Hill Whiteman, born in Wisconsin, is a member of the Oneida Tribe. Her poems have appeared in many journals, including *American Poetry Review*, *The Nation*, and *North American Review*, as well as anthologies of Native American verse. She currently teaches at the University of Wisconsin-Eau Claire.

Mitsuye Yamada was born in Kyushu, Japan and raised in Seattle, Washington, until the onset of WW II, when her family was relocated to an internment camp in Idaho. She has published several books of poems including *Camp Notes and Other Poems* (1976) and *Desert Run* (1988); received a National Endowment for the Arts Fellowship and a Yaddo Residency grant; and was featured in a PBS production, "Mitsuye and Nellie: Asian American Poets". She is a professor of English at Cypress College in California and the founder of Multicultural Women Writers of Orange County.

Mary Ann Caws, Distinguished Professor of English, French, and Comparative Literature in the Graduate School, City University of New York, has published four books and edited two collections. Her most recent book is *Women of Bloomsbury*. She lives in New York City.

Grace Glueck, a native of New York and graduate of New York University, was art news editor of *The New York Times* until 1991. Now an art critic for *The Observer*, she also contributes to mny art publications. As a long-time supporter of women's art, she has lectured and written extensively on the subject. Ms. Glueck is a frequent juror of art exhibitions, lecturer, and participant on radio and television talk shows. She co-authored *Brooklyn: People and Places, Past and Present* (1991) and is the author of *New York: The Painted City* (1992).

Oriole Farb Feshbach was born in New York City, received a B.A. from Sarah Lawrence College and an M.F.A. from the University of Massachusetts. She has taught at Amherst College and the University of Massachusetts and is an Art and Photography Editor of *The Massachusetts Review*. Ms. Feshbach has had many one-person exhibitions at museums, galleries, and academic institutions including the New Jersey State Museum, Mabel Douglass Library at Rutgers University, and Jersey City State College in New Jersey; the Mead Art Museum and Amherst College in Massachusetts; Mary Ryan Gallery, New York; Albright College and Bucknell University in Pennsylvania; and Wesleyan University, Connecticut. Her work is in the collections of The Museum of Modern Art, New York; Hartford Atheneum, Connecticut; Zimmerli Art Museum and Newark Museum, New Jersey; Museum of Fine Arts, Rose Art Museum, and the Smith College Museum of Art in Massachusetts; Lehigh University, Pennsylvania, and the New Britain Museum of American Art, Connecticut. She has received two New Jersey State Council of the Arts Fellowship Awards and has published *Vanitas Self-Portrait Book*, an artists book, 1988, and *Illuminations: Images for the poem "Asphodel: That Greeny Flower,"* 1991.

Claire Heimarck was born in Blue Earth, Minnesota. She received her B.A. from St. Olaf College, Minnesota and M.F.A. from Columbia University School of the Arts. She also studied with Henry Pearson at the New School, and Robert Beverly Hale at the Art Student's League in New York City. Ms. Heimarck's work has been featured in one-person exhibitions at the Johnson and Johnson World Headquarters in New Brunswick, New Jersey, The Interchurch Center, New York, and in several university galleries. Her work has received numerous awards in juried exhibitions. Her prints were included in the U.S.-Korea Exchange Exhibition sponsored by the Los Angeles Printmaking Society, and the monotype exhibition sponsored by the International Graphic Arts Foundation at the Sigma Gallery in New York. Ms. Heimarck was included in the New Jersey Arts Annual Exhibitions at the New Jersey State and the Noyes Museums; also Invitational exhibitions at the Jersey City Museum, the Aljira Gallery in Newark, and the Jan Weiss Gallery in New York.

Lucy D. Rosenfeld was born in New York City, and received a B.A. from Sarah Lawrence College. She is both an artist and author of books and videos on art and cultural history, including: *What's in a Painting, Introduction to Multicultural Art, Reading Pictures, Women Artists from Ancient to Modern Times* (a filmstrip), and a *A Complete Course in Drawing*, for which she also made drawings and collages. She is co-author and illustrator of *A Walker's Guidebook, Artwalks in New York* and the forthcoming *Art On Site*. Ms. Rosenfeld has shown her paintings and collages in one-person shows and group exhibitions at the Waverly Gallery in New York, the Provincetown Art Association, the Newark Public Library, and many other venues in New England and the tri-state area. She is currently at work on a six volume introduction to the history of Western art for classroom use.

List of Images

Acknowledgements and Permissions:

Adams, Jeanette, "For Gwen, My Mentor, My Friend," from *Say That the River Turns, a 70th Birthday Tribute to Gwendolyn Brooks*, Third World Press, Chicago, IL, 1987, © 1987 by the poet.

Atwood, Margaret, "Journey to the Interior," and "Repent" reprinted by permission of Margaret Atwood, © 1986, from *Selected Poems II*, Simon and Schuster, Inc., NY.

Berke, Judith, "The Returner" from *The American Poetry Review*, vol 19:5, August 1990, © and permission of the poet.

Brooks, Gwendolyn, "Sadie and Maud" from *Blacks*, The David Company, Chicago, IL, 1987; reprinted by permission of the poet.

Cerenio, Virginia, "the dream" from *Trespassing Innocence*, 1989, Kearny Street Workshop Press, San Francisco, 1989; © and permission of the poet.

Cervantes, Lorna Dee, "Como Lo Siento," reprinted by permission of Revista Chicano-Riquena, University of Houston, TX.

Chin, Marilyn, "The Narrow Roads of Oku," from *Dwarf Bamboo*, © 1987 by the poet, reprinted by permission of the poet.

Clampitt, Amy, "Amherst" from *Westward*, Alfred A. Knopf, NY, 1990; "The Reedbeds of the Hackensack" from *What the Light Was Like*," Alfred A. Knopf, 1986. Reprinted by permission of the poet.

Clifton, Lucille, "water, sign, woman," © 1991 by the poet, reprinted from *quilting: poems: 1987-1990* by Lucille Clifton, with permission of BOA Editions, Ltd., NY, and the author.

Cofer, Judith Ortiz, "Postcard Poem" reprinted from *Terms of Survival*, 1987, by permission of Arte Publico Press-University of Houston, TX.

Cooper, Jane, "The Green Notebook," © Jane Cooper; reprinted by permission of the poet.

DiPrima, Diane, "The Belltower" and "Limantour Beach II" reprinted by permission of the poet.

Doolittle, Hilda, "Sheltered Garden," and "Moonrise," from *H.D. Collected Poems, 1912-1944*, © 1982 by the Estate of Hilda Doolittle; reprinted by permission of New Directions Publishing Corp., NY.

Dove, Rita, "In the Museum" and "Your Death" from *Grace Notes, Poems*, by permission of W.W. Norton & Company, Inc., NY. "The Fish in the Stone" from *Museum*, © 1985 by the poet; reprinted by permission of Carnegie Mellon University Press.

Gallagher, Tess, "Second Language" © 1987 by the poet, reprinted from *Amplitude*, by permission of Graywolf Press, St. Paul, MN.

Graham, Jorie, "Erosion" reprinted from *The American Poetry Review*, Sept/October 1981 by permission of the poet.

Grosholz, Emily, "On the Loss of My Mother's Jewelry" from *The River Painter*, University of Illinois Press, 1984, reprinted by permission of the poet and the University of Illinois Press; "After Timaeus" from *Shores and Headlands*, © 1988, reprinted by permission of the poet and Princeton University Press, NJ.

Halley, Anne, "Fun House" and "Our Journey to Ghent"; from *Between Wars*, University of Massachusetts Press, 1964, and reprinted in Kenyon Review, 1982; © and permission by the poet

Harter, Penny, "Reading the Tea Leaves" from *Bluestones and Salt Hay: An Anthology of Contemporary New Jersey Poets*, © 1990 by Rutgers, The State University of New Jersey; reprinted by permission of the poet.

Harjo, Joy, "Hieroglyphic," © 1990 by the poet, reprinted from *In Mad Love and War*, Wesleyan University Press, by permission of University Press of New England.

Inez, Colette, "In Praise of Outlines" from *Folio*, American University Graduate Center, Washington, DC, 1988; reprinted by permission of the poet.

Johnson, Helene, "Trees at Night" from *Opportunity 3*, May 1925.

Keyishian, Marjorie, "Slow Runner" reprinted from *The Massachusetts Review*, Summer 1991, by permission of the poet.

Kumin, Maxine, "Whippoorwill," © 1971 by the poet; reprinted by permission of Curtis Brown, Ltd.;

Laing, Dilys, "Shopping List" and "Kwan Yin" from *The Collected Poems of Dilys Laing*, The Press of Case Western Reserve University, 1967; © and permission of David Laing.

Lauterbach, Ann, "Tuscan Visit (Simone Martini)," © 1991 by the poet, reprinted from *Clamor* by permission of Viking Penguin, a division of Penguin Books USA, Inc., NY.

Levertov, Denise, "A Blessing" from *Breathing the Water*, © 1987, and "The Room" from *Collected Earlier Poems 1940-1960*, © by Denise Levertov Goodman; reprinted by permission of New Directions Publishing Corp., NY.

Loy, Mina, "Brancusi's Golden Bird" and "Gertrude Stein" from *The Last Baedeker*, Jargon Society Press, 1982, by permission of the publisher.

Moore, Marianne, "What Are Years" from *Collected Poems of Marianne Moore*, © 1941, and renewed 1969, by the poet; reprinted by permission of Macmillan Publishing Company.

Back Cover:

typographic design: Barbara Bergeron

cover: MOG

Sources and Notes

Folio I

Jeanette Adams, "For Gwen, My Mentor, My Friend," volcanic cone of Orizaba in Mexico after A. von Humboldt; Pyramid of Cheops, Gaza; head of Queen Tiye, late reign of Menhotep II, Akhenaten Collection, Egyptian Museum, Berlin; *Hair Blossoms,*, Lloyd Sexton (1912-1990), c. 1941, o/c, private collection, Honolulu; portrait of Gwendolyn Brooks based on photograph by Roy Lewis.

Amy Clampitt, "Amherst," daguerreotype of Emily Dickinson by permission of the Trustees of Amherst College; image of Amy Clampitt based on photograph by Virginia Schendler. Fascicle 20, p. 441 from The Manuscript Books of Emily Dickinson, Volume 1, 1981, Belknap Press of Harvard University Press, "by permission of the Houghton Library."

In Amy Clampitt's poem "The Reedbeds of the Hackensack," "Allusions to and/or borrowings from the poems of William Carlos Williams, Dante, Milton, Keats, and Shakespeare will be noted, which may be regarded as a last-ditch effort to associate the landscape familiarly known as the Jersey Meadows with the tradition of elegiac poetry."

Dilys Lang, "Kwan Yin," *Gakko-Bosatsu* Tempyo Period (708-781) photograph by Rokumei-So; *Madonna and Child*, Luca della Robbia, c. 1450, Samuel H. Kress Collection, Philbrook Art Center, Tulsa, Oklahoma.

Mina Loy, "Gertrude Stein," based on photograph of Gertrude Stein, 1937, by Imogen Cunningham; and photograph of Irène Curie based on photograph of Irène and Frederic Joliet-Curie, 1945, by Henri Cartier-Bresson. The Madame Curie metaphor originally appeared as the opening epigraph of a letter on Gertrude Stein addressed to Ford Madox Ford.

Mina Loy, "Brancusi's Golden Bird," *Bird in Space*, by Constantin Brancusi, 1919, bronze, from the collection of the Museum of Modern Art, New York; gold mask of Tutankhamun. The poem first appeared with T.S. Eliot's "The Waste Land" in *Dial* (November 1922) and was reprinted in the catalogue for Brancusi's exhibitions in 1926 and 1927.

Joyce Carol Oates, "Homage to Virginia Woolf," *Virginia Stephen*, by G. C. Beresford, 1903, National Portrait Gallery, London.

Folio II

Marilyn Chin's poem "The Narrow Roads of Oku" refers in detail to the journal of Matsuo Basho, the 17th-century Haiku poet of Japan. His revered book, *Oku no hasamichi* has been translated by Sam Hamill as *The Narrow Road to the Interior. Oku* means "within" and *hasamichi* means "path" or "narrow road." The title can thus mean both the narrow road to the mountainous interior or the path to one's spiritual center.